Developing Microservices with Node.js

Learn to develop efficient and scalable microservices for server-side programming in Node.js using this hands-on guide

David Gonzalez

[PACKT] open source *
PUBLISHING community experience distilled

BIRMINGHAM - MUMBAI

Developing Microservices with Node.js

First published: April 2016

Production reference: 1220416

Published by Packt Publishing Ltd.
Livery Place
35 Livery Street
Birmingham B3 2PB, UK.

ISBN 978-1-78588-740-6

www.packtpub.com

Credits

Author
David Gonzalez

Reviewer
Kishore Kumar Yekkanti

Commissioning Editor
Veena Pagare

Acquisition Editor
Divya Poojari

Content Development Editor
Abhishek Jadhav

Technical Editor
Pranil Pathare

Copy Editor
Vibha Shukla

Project Coordinator
Judie Jose

Proofreader
Safis Editing

Indexer
Monica Ajmera Mehta

Production Coordinator
Arvindkumar Gupta

Cover Work
Arvindkumar Gupta

About the Author

David Gonzalez is a language-agnostic software engineer working in financial services for a number of years, trying to find solutions for the right level of abstraction and learning how to get the right balance between *too concrete* and *too abstract*.

He studied in Spain, but soon moved to the wider and more interesting market of Dublin, where he has been living since 2011. David is currently working as an independent consultant in the FinTech sector. The URL to his Linkedin account is `https://ie.linkedin.com/in/david-gonzalez-737b7383`.

He loves experimenting with new technologies and paradigms in order to get the broader picture of the complex world of software development.

To my wife, Ester, thanks for your unconditional support in every single aspect of my life.

To my unborn daughter, Elena, may the life give you all the happiness that you are bringing to your parents.

About the Reviewer

Kishore Kumar Yekkanti is an experienced professional who has worked across various domains and technologies over the past ten years. He is passionate about eliminating the waste during the software development. Kishore is a huge contributor to and follower of agile principles. He is a full-stack developer who wants to build the end-to-end systems, and a polyglot programmer. His current focus is on scaling microservices in highly distributed applications that are deployed using container-based systems (Docker) on cloud. He has worked as the lead/principal engineer for many well-known companies such as Thoughtworks, CurrencyFair, and others, where he lead the teams to attain nirvana through microservices.

> For my partner and best friend Jyothsna, and my daughter, Dhruti, who continues to humour me despite of my crazy schedules.

www.PacktPub.com

eBooks, discount offers, and more

Did you know that Packt offers eBook versions of every book published, with PDF and ePub files available? You can upgrade to the eBook version at www.PacktPub.com and as a print book customer, you are entitled to a discount on the eBook copy. Get in touch with us at customercare@packtpub.com for more details.

At www.PacktPub.com, you can also read a collection of free technical articles, sign up for a range of free newsletters and receive exclusive discounts and offers on Packt books and eBooks.

https://www2.packtpub.com/books/subscription/packtlib

Do you need instant solutions to your IT questions? PacktLib is Packt's online digital book library. Here, you can search, access, and read Packt's entire library of books.

Why subscribe?

- Fully searchable across every book published by Packt
- Copy and paste, print, and bookmark content
- On demand and accessible via a web browser

Table of Contents

Preface

This book is a hands-on guide to start writing microservices using Node.js and the most modern frameworks, especially Seneca and PM2. In the chapters, we will discuss how to design, build, test, and deploy microservices using the best practices. We will also discuss a valuable lesson: how to make the right level of compromise in order to avoid over-designing and get the business requirements aligned with the technical solutions.

What this book covers

Chapter 1, *Microservices Architecture*, discusses the pros and cons of microservices-oriented architectures. It will be the foundation for the rest of the book.

Chapter 2, *Microservices in Node.js – Seneca and PM2 Alternatives*, introduces Node.js, Seneca, and PM2. In it, we will discuss the structure of a Node.js application and how to run it using PM2. We will also dive into a few alternatives to Seneca and PM2.

Chapter 3, *From the Monolith to Microservices*, covers how to tackle the organic growth (unplanned software changes) using microservices. We will also talk about how to split a monolithic application into microservices.

Chapter 4, *Writing Your First Microservice in Node.js*, explains how to write our first microservice.

Chapter 5, *Security and Traceability*, covers how security and traceability are two important characteristics of modern systems. We need to keep the information secure and the actions traceable. In this chapter, we will discuss how to do it using Seneca.

Chapter 6, Testing and Documenting Node.js Microservices, introduces using the main frameworks for testing on Node.js: Mocha and Chai. We will also make use of Sinon (another framework) to mock services. Swagger will be our choice for documenting microservices.

Chapter 7, Monitoring Microservices, covers using PM2 to monitor our microservices. We will use it along with Keymetrics to get the maximum benefit of such an advanced tool.

Chapter 8, Deploying Microservices, explains how, using PM2, we are going to learn to deploy microservices in our different environments, managing our ecosystem of applications with a single command and reducing the overhead introduced by the microservices architecture. We will also discuss Docker, one of the most advanced systems to deploy applications not only in Node.js, but also in general applications.

What you need for this book

In order to follow the book, we are going to need to install Node.js, PM2 (it is a package that is installed through npm), and MongoDB.

We will also need an editor. Personally, I use Atom, but any general purpose editor should be enough.

Who this book is for

This book is for developers that have some experience with Node.js but want to learn about Seneca and microservices. It is 70% practice-oriented (as we will be writing a lot of code), but it also is 30% theory, based on the code created that will help the reader to apply the exposed patterns to new software.

Conventions

In this book, you will find a number of text styles that distinguish between different kinds of information. Here are some examples of these styles and an explanation of their meaning.

Code words in text, database table names, folder names, filenames, file extensions, pathnames, dummy URLs, user input, and Twitter handles are shown as follows: "We know that the input parameter is a `PaymentRequest` instance."

A block of code is set as follows:

```
public interface PaymentService {
  PaymentResponse processPayment(PaymentRequest request) throws
    MyBusinessException;
}
```

When we wish to draw your attention to a particular part of a code block, the relevant lines or items are set in bold:

```
function() {
  sinon.stub(Math, "random");
  rollDice();
  console.log(Math.random.calledWith());
});
after(function(){
  Math.random.restore();
});
```

Any command-line input or output is written as follows:

```
node index.js

npm start
```

New terms and **important words** are shown in bold. Words that you see on the screen, for example, in menus or dialog boxes, appear in the text like this: "In this case, I have used Chrome and the console shows an **Uncaught TypeError: Cannot set property 'innerText' of null** error in line 7."

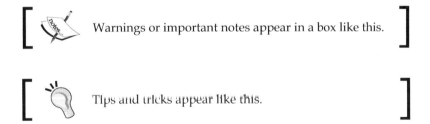

Warnings or important notes appear in a box like this.

Tips and tricks appear like this.

Reader feedback

Feedback from our readers is always welcome. Let us know what you think about this book—what you liked or disliked. Reader feedback is important for us as it helps us develop titles that you will really get the most out of.

To send us general feedback, simply e-mail feedback@packtpub.com, and mention the book's title in the subject of your message.

If there is a topic that you have expertise in and you are interested in either writing or contributing to a book, see our author guide at www.packtpub.com/authors.

Customer support

Now that you are the proud owner of a Packt book, we have a number of things to help you to get the most from your purchase.

Downloading the example code

You can download the example code files for this book from your account at http://www.packtpub.com. If you purchased this book elsewhere, you can visit http://www.packtpub.com/support and register to have the files e-mailed directly to you.

You can download the code files by following these steps:

1. Log in or register to our website using your e-mail address and password.
2. Hover the mouse pointer on the **SUPPORT** tab at the top.
3. Click on **Code Downloads & Errata**.
4. Enter the name of the book in the **Search** box.
5. Select the book for which you're looking to download the code files.
6. Choose from the drop-down menu where you purchased this book from.
7. Click on **Code Download**.

You can also download the code files by clicking on the **Code Files** button on the book's webpage at the Packt Publishing website. This page can be accessed by entering the book's name in the **Search** box. Please note that you need to be logged in to your Packt account.

Once the file is downloaded, please make sure that you unzip or extract the folder using the latest version of:

*   WinRAR / 7-Zip for Windows
*   Zipeg / iZip / UnRarX for Mac
*   7-Zip / PeaZip for Linux

Errata

Although we have taken every care to ensure the accuracy of our content, mistakes do happen. If you find a mistake in one of our books—maybe a mistake in the text or the code—we would be grateful if you could report this to us. By doing so, you can save other readers from frustration and help us improve subsequent versions of this book. If you find any errata, please report them by visiting http://www.packtpub. com/submit-errata, selecting your book, clicking on the **Errata Submission Form** link, and entering the details of your errata. Once your errata are verified, your submission will be accepted and the errata will be uploaded to our website or added to any list of existing errata under the Errata section of that title.

To view the previously submitted errata, go to https://www.packtpub.com/books/ content/support and enter the name of the book in the search field. The required information will appear under the **Errata** section.

Piracy

Piracy of copyrighted material on the Internet is an ongoing problem across all media. At Packt, we take the protection of our copyright and licenses very seriously. If you come across any illegal copies of our works in any form on the Internet, please provide us with the location address or website name immediately so that we can pursue a remedy.

Please contact us at copyright@packtpub.com with a link to the suspected pirated material.

We appreciate your help in protecting our authors and our ability to bring you valuable content.

Questions

If you have a problem with any aspect of this book, you can contact us at questions@packtpub.com, and we will do our best to address the problem.

1
Microservices Architecture

Microservices are becoming more and more popular. Nowadays, pretty much every engineer on a green field project should be considering using microservices in order to improve the quality of the systems they build. They should know the architectural principles involving such systems. We will expose the difference between microservices and **Service-Oriented Architecture** (**SOA**). We will also introduce a great platform to write microservices, **Node.js**, which will allow us to create high-performing microservices with very little effort.

In this chapter, you will learn about microservices from the architectural point of view:

- What are microservices?
- Microservice-oriented architectures
- Key benefits
- SOA versus Microservices
- Why Node.js?

Need for microservices

The world of software development has evolved quickly in the past 40 years. One of the key points of this evolution has been the size of these systems. From the days of MS-DOS, we have taken a hundred-fold leap into our present systems. This growth in size creates a need for better ways of organizing code and software components. Usually, when a company grows due to business needs, known as **organic growth**, the software is organized on a monolithic architecture as it is the easiest and quickest way of building software. After few years (or even months), adding new features becomes harder due to the coupled nature of the created software.

Monolithic software

The natural trend for new high-tech companies such as Amazon or Netflix is building their new software using microservices, which is the ideal scenario: they get a huge advantage of microservices-oriented software (through out this book, you will learn how) in order to scale up their new products without a big effort. The problem is that not all companies can plan their software upfront. Instead of planning, these companies build software based on the organic growth experienced: few software components group business flows by affinity. It is not rare to see companies with two big software components: the user-facing website and the internal administration tools. This is usually known as a **monolithic software architecture**.

Some of these companies face big problems when trying to scale the engineering teams. It is hard to coordinate teams that build, deploy, and maintain a single software component. Clashes on releases and reintroduction of bugs are a common problem that drains a large chunk of energy from the teams. One of the solution to this problem (it comes with benefits) is to split the monolithic software into microservices so that the teams are able to specialize in a few smaller modules and autonomous and isolated software components that can be versioned, updated, and deployed without interfering with the rest of the systems of the company.

Splitting the monolith into microservices enables the engineering team to create isolated and autonomous units of work that are highly specialized in a given task such as sending e-mails, processing card payments, and so on.

Microservices in the real world

Microservices are small software components that are specialized in one task and work together to achieve a higher-level task. Forget about software for a second and think about how a company works. When someone applies for a job in a company, he applies for a given position: software engineer, system administrator, office manager. The reason for this can be summarized in one word: specialization. If you are used to work as a software engineer, you will get better with the experience and add more value to the company. The fact that you don't know how to deal with a customer, won't affect your performance as that is not your area of expertise and will hardly add any value to your day-to-day work.

 Specialization is often the key to improve the efficiency. Doing one thing and doing it right is one of the mantras of software development.

A microservice is an autonomous unit of work that can execute one task without interfering with other parts of the system, similar to what a job position is to a company. This has a number of benefits that can be used in favor of the engineering team in order to help scale the systems of a company.

Nowadays, hundreds of systems are built using microservices-oriented architectures, as follows:

- **Netflix**: This is one of the most popular streaming services, it has built an entire ecosystem of applications that collaborate in order to provide a reliable and scalable streaming system used across the globe.

- **Spotify**: This is one of the leading music streaming services in the world, it has built this application using microservices. Every single widget of the application (which is a website exposed as a desktop app using Chromium Embedded Framework) is a different microservice that can be updated individually.

Microservice-oriented architectures

Microservices-oriented architectures have some particularities that makes them desirable for any mid/large-sized company that wants to keep their IT systems resilient and in scale up/down-ready status.

How is it better?

They are not the holy grail of software engineering, but, when handled with care, they become the perfect approach to solve most of the big problems faced by tech-dependent companies.

It is important to keep the key principles of the microservices-oriented architecture's design in mind, such as resilience, composability, elasticity, and so on; otherwise, you could end up with a monolithic application split across different machines that produces problems rather than an elegant solution.

Shortcomings

There is also some criticism around microservices-oriented architectures, as they introduce some problems to deal with, such as latency, traceability, and configuration management that are not present with monolithic-based software. Some of the problems are described as follows:

- **Network latency**: Microservices have a distributed nature so that network latency has to be accounted for

- **Operations overhead**: More servers indicate more maintenance

- **Eventual consistency**: On highly transactional systems, we need to factor into implementation the fact that the data could be inconsistent during a period of time (we will talk about it later in this chapter)

In general, engineers should try to evaluate the pros and cons of this approach and make a decision on whether to use microservices or not in order to fit the business needs.

Microservices-oriented architectures have some particularities that need to be taken into consideration. When a software engineer is writing monolithic software, there are some problems that are completely overlooked due to the nature of the software being built.

For example, imagine that our software needs to send e-mails. In a monolithic software, we would just add the functionality to the core of the application. We might even choose to create a dedicated module to deal with e-mails (which seems like a good idea). Now, imagine that we are creating a microservice and, instead of adding a functionality to a big software artifact, we create a dedicated service that can be deployed and versioned independently. In this case, we will have an extra step that we didn't have to take into consideration, the **network latency**, to reach the new microservice.

In the preceding example, no matter what approach (monolithic or microservices) you are taking to build the software, is not a big deal; for example, if an e-mail is lost, it is not the end of the world. As per definition, the e-mail delivery is not guaranteed, so our application will still work, although we might receive a few complaints from our customers.

Key design principles

There are a few key design principles that need to be taken into consideration when building microservices. There is no golden rule and, as microservices are a recent concept, sometimes there is even a lack of consensus on what practices to follow. In general, we can assume the following design principles:

- Microservices are business units that model the company processes.

- They are smart endpoints that contain the business logic and communicate using simple channels and protocols.

- Microservices-oriented architectures are decentralized by definition. This helps to build robust and resilient software.

Business units, no components

One of the most enjoyable sides of software engineering is creating a new project. This is where you can apply all your creativity, try new architectural concepts, frameworks, or methodologies. Unfortunately, it is not a common situation in a mature company. Usually, what we do is create new components inside the existing software. One of the best design principles that you can follow when creating new components is keeping the coupling as low as possible with the rest of the software, so that it works as an independent unit.

 Keeping a low level of coupling allows a software component to be converted into a microservice with little to no effort.

Consider a real-world example: the application of your company now needs to be able to process payments.

The logical decision here would be creating a new module that knows how to deal with the chosen payment provider (credit cards, PayPal, and so on) and allows us to keep all the payment-related business logic inside of it. Let's define the interface in the following code:

```
public interface PaymentService {
   PaymentResponse processPayment(PaymentRequest request) throws
     MyBusinessException;
}
```

This simple interface can be understood by everyone, but it is the key when moving towards microservices. We have encapsulated all the business knowledge behind an interface so that we could theoretically switch the payment provider without affecting the rest of the application—the implementation details are hidden from the outer world.

The following is what we know until now:

- We know the method name, therefore, we know how to invoke the service
- The method could throw an exception of the `MyBusinessException` type, forcing the calling code to deal with it
- We know that the input parameter is a `PaymentRequest` instance
- The response is a known object

We have created a highly cohesive and loosely coupled business unit. Let's justify this affirmation in the following:

- **Highly cohesive**: All the code inside the payments module will do only one thing, that is, deal with payments and all the aspects of calling a third-party service (connection handling, response codes, and so on), such as a debit card processor.

- **Loosely coupled**: What happens if, for some reason, we need to switch to a new payment processor? Is there any information bleeding out of the interface? Would we need to change the calling code due to changes in the contract? The answer is no. The implementation of the payment service interface will always be a modular unit of work.

The following diagram shows how a system composed of many components gets one of them (payment service) stripped out into a microservice:

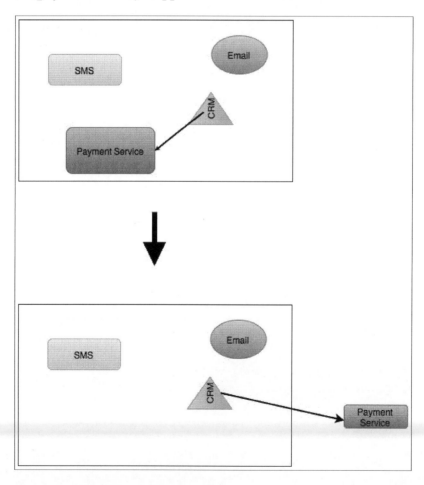

Once this module is implemented, we will be able to process the payments and our monolithic application will have another functionality that could be a good candidate to extract into a microservice.

Now, we can rollout new versions of the payment service, as long as the interface does not change, as well as the contract with the rest of the world (our system or third parties), hasn't changed. That is why it is so important to keep the implementation independent from interfacing, even though the language does not provide support for interfaces.

We can also scale up and deploy as many payment services as we require so that we can satisfy the business needs without unnecessarily scaling the rest of the application that might not be under pressure.

Downloading the example code

You can download the example code files for this book from your account at `http://www.packtpub.com`. If you purchased this book elsewhere, you can visit `http://www.packtpub.com/support` and register to have the files e-mailed directly to you.

You can download the code files by following these steps:

- Log in or register to our website using your e-mail address and password.
- Hover the mouse pointer on the **SUPPORT** tab at the top.
- Click on **Code Downloads & Errata**.
- Enter the name of the book in the **Search** box.
- Select the book for which you're looking to download the code files.
- Choose from the drop-down menu where you purchased this book from.
- Click on **Code Download**.

You can also download the code files by clicking on the **Code Files** button on the book's webpage at the Packt Publishing website. This page can be accessed by entering the book's name in the **Search** box. Please note that you need to be logged in to your Packt account.

Once the file is downloaded, please make sure that you unzip or extract the folder using the latest version of:

- WinRAR / 7-Zip for Windows
- Zipeg / iZip / UnRarX for Mac
- 7-Zip / PeaZip for Linux

Smart services, dumb communication pipes

Hyper Text Transfer Protocol (HTTP) is one of the best things to have ever happened to the Internet. Imagine a protocol that was designed to be state-less, but was hacked through the use of cookies in order to hold the status of the client. This was during the age of Web 1.0, when no one was talking about REST APIs or mobile apps. Let's see an example of an HTTP request:

```
HTTP/1.1 200 OK
Date: Mon, 23 May 2005 22:38:34 GMT
Server: Apache/1.3.3.7 (Unix) (Red-Hat/Linux)
Last-Modified: Wed, 08 Jan 2003 23:11:55 GMT
ETag: "3f80f-1b6-3e1cb03b"
Content-Type: text/html; charset=UTF-8
Content-Length: 138
Accept-Ranges: bytes
Connection: close
```

As you can see, it is a *human readable* protocol that does not need to be explained in order to be understood.

Nowadays, it is broadly understood that HTTP is not confined to be used in the Web, and as it was designed, it is now used as a general purpose protocol to transfer data from one endpoint to another. HTTP is all you need for the communication between microservices: a protocol to transfer data and recover from transmission errors (when possible).

In the past few years, especially within the enterprise world, there has been an effort to create smart communication mechanisms such as **BPEL**. BPEL stands for **Business Process Execution Language**, and instead of focusing on communication actions, it focuses on actions around business steps.

This introduces some level of complexity in the communication protocol and makes the business logic of the application bleed into it from the endpoints, causing some level of coupling between the endpoints.

The business logic should stay within the endpoints and not bleed into the communication channel so that the system can be easily tested and scaled. The lesson learned through the years is that the communication layer must be a plain and simple protocol that ensures the transmission of the data and the endpoints (microservices).These endpoints should embed into their implementation the fact that a service could be down for a period of time (this is called resilience, we will talk about this later in this chapter) or the network could cause communication issues.

HTTP usually is the most used protocol when building microservices-oriented software but another interesting option that needs to be explored is the use of queues, such as Rabbit MQ and Kafka, to facilitate the communication between endpoints.

The queueing technology provides a clean approach to manage the communication in a buffered way, encapsulating the complexities of acknowledging messages on highly transactional systems.

Decentralization

One of the major cons of monolithic applications is the centralization of everything on a single (or few) software components and databases. This, more often than not, leads to huge data stores that needs to be replicated and scaled according to the needs of the company and centralized governance of the flows.

Microservices aim for decentralization. Instead of having a huge database, why not split the data according to the business units explained earlier?

Some of the readers could use the transactionality as one of the main reasons for not doing it. Consider the following scenario:

1. A customer buys an item in our microservices-oriented online shop.
2. When paying for the item, the system issues the following calls:
    1. A call to the financial system of the company to create a transaction with the payment.
    2. A call to the warehouse system to dispatch the book.
    3. A call to the mailing system to subscribe the customer to the newsletter.

In a monolithic software, all the calls would be wrapped in a transaction, so if, for some reason, any of the calls fails, the data on the other calls won't be persisted in the database.

When you learn about designing databases, one of the first and the most important principles are summarized by the **ACID** acronym:

- **Atomicity**: Each transaction will be all or nothing. If one part fails, no changes are persisted on the database.

- **Consistency**: Changes to the data through transactions need to guarantee its consistency.

- **Isolation**: The result of concurrent execution of transactions results in a system state that would be obtained if the transactions were executed serially.

- **Durability**: Once the transaction is committed, the data persists.

On a microservices-oriented software, the ACID principle is not guaranteed globally. Microservices will commit the transaction locally, but there are no mechanisms that can guarantee a 100% integrity of the global transaction. It would be possible to dispatch the book without processing the payment, unless we factor in specific rules to prevent it.

On a microservices-oriented architecture, the transactionality of the data is not guaranteed, so we need to factor the failure into the implementation. A way to solve (although, workaround is a more appropriate word) this problem is decentralizing the governance and data storage.

When building microservices, we need to embed in the design, the fact that one or more components could fail and degrade the functionality according to the availability of the software.

Let's take a look at the following diagram:

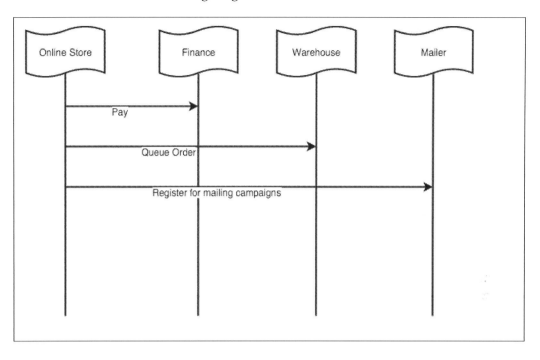

This diagram represents the sequence of execution on a monolithic software. A sequential list of calls that, no matter what, are going to be executed following the ACID principle: either all the calls (transactions) succeed or none of them do.

This is only possible as the framework and database engine designers have developed the concept of transactions to guarantee the transactionality of the data.

When working with microservices, we need to account for what the engineers call eventual consistency. After a partial fail on a transaction, each microservice instance should store the information required to recover the transaction so that the information will be eventually consistent. Following the previous example, if we send the book without processing the payment, the payment gateway will have a failed transaction that someone will process later on, making the data consistent again.

The best way to solve this problem is decentralizing the governance. Every endpoint should be able to take a local decision that affects the global scope of the transaction. We will talk more about this subject in *Chapter 3, From the Monolith to Microservices*.

Technology alignment

When building a new software, there is always a concept that every developer should keep in mind: **standards**.

Standards guarantee that your service will be technologically independent so that it will be easy to build the integrations using a different programming language or technologies.

One of the advantages of modeling a system with microservices is that we can choose the right technology for the right job so that we can be quite efficient when tackling problems. When building monolithic software, it is fairly hard to combine technologies like we can do with microservices. Usually, in a monolithic software, we are tied to the technology that we choose in the beginning.

Java Remote Method Invocation (RMI) is one example of the non-standard protocols that should be avoided if you want your system to be open to new technologies. It is a great way of connecting software components written in Java, but the developers will struggle (if not fail) to invoke an RMI method using Node.js. This will tie our architecture to a given language, which from the microservices point of view, will kill one of the most interesting advantages: **technology heterogeneity**.

How small is too small?

Once we have decided to model our system as a set of microservices, there is always one question that needs an answer: *how small is too small?*

The answer is always tricky and probably disappointing: *it depends*.

The right size of the microservices in a given system depends on the structure of the company as well as the ability to create software components that are easily manageable by a small team of developers. It also depends on the technical needs.

Imagine a system that receives and processes banking files; as you are probably aware, all the payments between banks are sent in files with a specific known format (such as **Single Euro Payments Area (SEPA)** for Euro payments). One of the particularities of this type of systems is the large number of different files that the system needs to know how to process.

The first approach for this problem is tackling it from the microservices point of view, separating it from any other service creating a unit of work, and creating one microservice for each type of file. It will enable us to be able to rollout modifications for the existing file processors without interfering with the rest of the system. It will also enable us to keep processing files even though one of the services is experiencing problems.

The microservices should be as small as needed, but keep in mind that every microservice adds an overhead to the operations team that needs to manage a new service. Try to answer the question *how small is too small?* in terms of manageability, scalability, and specialization. The microservice should be small enough to be managed and scaled up (or down) quickly without affecting the rest of the system, by a single person; and it should do only one thing.

 As a general rule, a microservice should be small enough to be completely rewritten in a sprint.

Key benefits

In the previous topic, we talked about what a microservices-oriented architecture is. I also exposed the design principles that I have learned from experience, as well as showed a few benefits of this type of architecture.

Now, it is time to outline these key benefits and show how they will help us to improve the quality of our software, as well as be able to quickly accommodate the new business requirements.

Resilience

Resilience is defined in Wikipedia as *the ability of a system to cope with change*. I like to think about resilience as the *ability of a system to gracefully recover from an exception* (transitory hardware failure, unexpectedly high network latency, and so on) or a stress period without affecting the performance of the system once the situation has been resolved.

Although it sounds simple, when building microservices-oriented software, the source of problems broadens due to the distributed nature of the system, sometimes making it hard (or even impossible) to prevent all abnormal situations.

Resilience is the ability to gracefully recover from errors. It also adds another level of complexity: if one microservice is experiencing problems, can we prevent a general failure? Ideally, we should build our system in a way that the service response is degraded instead of resulting in a general failure, although this is not always easy.

Scalability

Nowadays, one of the common problems in companies is the scalability of the systems. If you have worked on a monolithic software before, I am sure that you have experienced capacity problems at some point, alongside the growth of the company.

Usually, these problems are not across all the layers or subsystems of the application. There is always a subsystem or service that performs significantly slower than the rest, causing the entire application to fail if it is not able to cope with the demand.

The following diagram describes how a microservice can be scaled up (two mailing services) without interfering with the rest of the system:

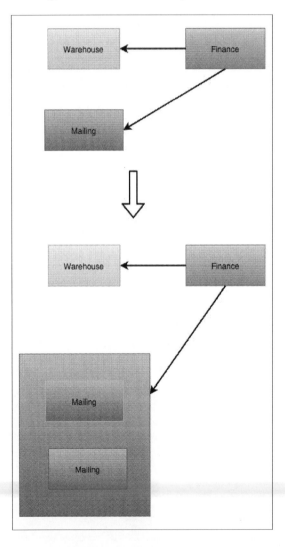

An example of these weak points in the world of car insurance is the service that calculates the quote for a given list of risk factors. Would it make sense to scale the full application just to satisfy the demand for this particular part? If the answer that you have in mind is *no*, you are one step closer to embracing microservices. Microservices enable you to scale parts of the system as the demand ramps up for a particular area of it.

If our insurance system was a microservice-oriented software, the only thing needed to resolve the high demand for quote calculations would've been to spawn more instances of the microservice (or microservices) responsible for their calculation. Please bear in mind that scaling up services could add an overhead for operating them.

Technology heterogeneity

The world of software is changing every few months. New languages are coming to the industry as a de facto standard for a certain type of systems. A few years ago, Ruby on Rails appeared at the scene and rose as one of the most used web frameworks for new projects in 2013. Golang (a language created by Google) is becoming a trend nowadays as it combines huge performance with an elegant and simple syntax that can be learned by anyone with some experience in another programming language in a matter of days.

In the past, I have used Python and Java as successful alternatives to write microservices.

Java especially, since Spring Boot was released, is an attractive technology stack to write agile (to write and operate) microservices.

Django, is also a powerful framework on Python to write microservices. Being very similar to Ruby on Rails, it automates database migrations and makes the creation of **CRUD (Create Read Update Delete)** services an incredibly easy task.

Node.js took the advantage of a well-known language, JavaScript, to create a new server-side stack that is changing the way engineers create new software.

So, what is wrong in combining all of them? In all fairness, it is an advantage: *we can choose the right tool for the right job*.

Microservices-oriented architectures enable you to do it, as long as the integration technologies are standard. As you learned before, a microservice is a *small and independent piece of software that can operate by itself.*

The following diagram shows how the microservices hide data storage/gathering, having only the communication points in common—making them a good example of low coupling (one service implementation change won't interfere with any other service):

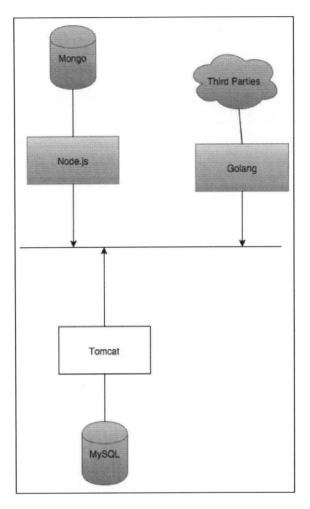

We have talked about performance earlier. There are always parts of our systems that are under more pressure than others. With modern multicore CPUs, parallel (concurrent) programming could solve some of these performance issues, however, Node.js is not a good language to parallelize tasks. We could choose to rewrite the microservice under pressure using a more appropriate language, such as Erlang, to manage concurrency in a more elegant way. It should take no more than two weeks to do it.

There is a downside to using multiple technologies on the same system: the developers and system administrators need to know all (or a few) of them. Companies that embraced microservices usually try to stick with one core technology (in this book, we will be using Node.js) and some auxiliary technologies (although we will be using Docker to manage the deployments, we could use Capistrano or Fabricator to manage the releases).

Replaceability

Replaceability is the ability to change one component of a system without interfering with how the system behaves.

When talking about software, replaceability comes along with low coupling. We should be writing our microservices in a way that the internal logic will not be exposed to the calling services so that the clients of a given service do not need to know about how it is implemented, just the interface. Let's take a look at the following example. It is written in Java as we only need to see the interface to identify the pitfalls:

```java
public interface GeoIpService {
  /**
   * Checks if an IP is in the country given by an ISO code.
   **/
  boolean isIn(String ip, String isoCode) throws
    SOAPFaultException;
}
```

This interface, at first look, is self explanatory. It checks whether a given IP is in a given country and throws a SOAPFaultException, which is a big problem.

If we build the client that consumes this service, factoring into their logic, capture, and processing of the SoapFaultException, we are exposing internal implementation details to the outer world and making it hard to replace the GeoIpService interface. Also, the fact that we are creating a service related to a part of our application logic is an indication of the creation of a **bounded context**: a highly cohesive service or set of services that work together to achieve one purpose.

Independence

No matter how hard we try, the human brain is not designed to solve complex problems. The most efficient mode of functioning for the human brain is one thing at the time so that we *break down complex problems into smaller ones.* Microservices-oriented architectures should follow this approach: all the services should be independent and interact through the interface up to a point that they can be developed by different groups of engineers without any interaction, aside from agreeing the interfaces. This will enable a company adopting microservices to scale up, or down, the engineering teams, depending on the business needs, making the business agile in responding to peaks of demand or periods of quietness.

Why is replaceability important?

In a previous section, we talked about the right size of a microservice. As a general rule of thumb, a team should be able to rewrite and deploy a microservice in a sprint. The reason behind it is the **technical debt**.

I would define technical debt as the deviation from the original technical design to deliver the expected functionality within a planned deadline. Some of these sacrifices or wrong assumptions often lead to poorly written software that needs to be completely refactored or rewritten.

In the preceding example, the interface is exposing to the outer world the fact that we are using **SOAP** to call a web service, but we will need to change the code on the client side as a REST client has certainly nothing to do with SOAP exceptions.

Easy to deploy

Microservices should be easy to deploy.

Being software developers, we are well aware that a lot of things could go wrong, preventing a software from being deployed.

Microservices, as stated before, should be easy to deploy for a number of reasons, as stated in the following list:

- Small amount of business logic (remember the *two weeks re-write from scratch* rule of thumb) leading into simpler deployments.
- Microservices are autonomous units of work, so upgrading a service is a contained problem on a complex system. No need to re-deploy the entire system.

- Infrastructure and configuration on microservices architectures should be automated as much as possible. Later in the book, we will learn how to use Docker to deploy microservices and what are the benefits over the traditional deployment techniques are.

SOA versus microservices

Service-Oriented Architectures (**SOA**) has been around for a number of years. SOA is a great principle to design software. They are self-contained components providing services to other components. As we agreed before, it is all about maintaining low coupling on the different modules of the system as if it was a puzzle so that we can replace the pieces without causing a big impact on the overall system.

In principle, SOA looks very similar to microservices architectures. So what is the difference?

Microservices are fine-grained SOA components. In other words, a single SOA component can be decomposed in a number of microservices that can work together in order to provide the same level of functionality:

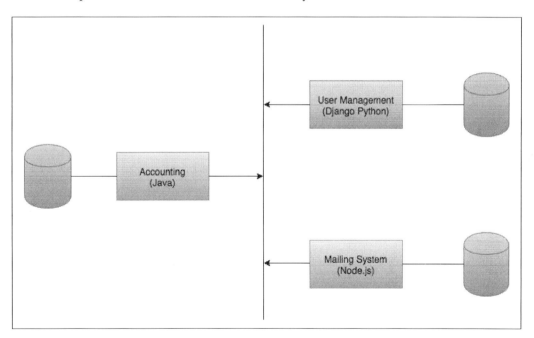

[Microservices are fine-grained SOA components.
They are lightweight services with a narrow focus.]

Another difference between microservices and SOA is the technologies used for interconnecting and writing the services.

J2EE is a technology stack that was designed to write SOA architectures as it enforced enterprise standards. Java Naming and Directory Interface, Enterprise Java Beans, and **Enterprise Service Bus (ESB)** were the ecosystems where SOA applications were built and maintained. Although ESB is a standard, very few engineers who graduated after 2005 have heard about ESB, even fewer have used it, and nowadays the modern frameworks such as Ruby on Rails do not even consider such complex pieces of software.

On the other hand, microservices enforce the use of standards (such as HTTP) that are broadly known and broadly interoperable. We can choose the right language or tool to build a component (microservice) following one of the key benefits explained earlier in this chapter, in the *Technology heterogeneity* section.

Aside from the technology stack and the size of the services, there is an even bigger difference between SOA and microservices: the domain model. Earlier in this chapter, we have talked about decentralization. Decentralization of the governance, but, moreover, decentralization of the data. In a microservices-based software, every microservice should store its own data locally, isolating the domain models to a single service; whereas, on an SOA oriented-software, the data is usually stored in a few big databases and the services share the domain models.

Why Node.js?

A few years ago, I didn't believe in Node.js. To me, it was a trend more than a real tool to solve problems… JavaScript in the server? That didn't look right. In all fairness, I didn't even like JavaScript. Then, the modern frameworks such as jQuery or Angular.js came to the rescue. They solved one of the problems, which was the cross-browser compatibility. Where before we needed to factor in at least three different browsers, after jQuery all this logic was nicely encapsulated in a library so that we didn't need to worry about compatibility as long as we followed the jQuery documentation.

Then, JavaScript became more popular. Suddenly, all the internal tools were written with **Single-Page Application (SPA)** frameworks with a heavy usage of JavaScript, therefore, the majority of developers nowadays, one way or another, are proficient in JavaScript.

Then, someone decided to take JavaScript out of the browser, which was a great idea. Rhino, Node.js, and Nashorn are examples of runtimes that can execute standalone JavaScript. Some of them can even interact with the Java code, enabling the developer to import Java classes into a JavaScript program, which gives you the access to an endless set of frameworks already written in Java.

Let's focus on **Node.js**. Node.js is the perfect candidate for microservices-oriented architectures for a number of reasons, as stated in the following list:

- Easy to learn (although it can be hard to master)
- Easy to scale
- Highly testable
- Easy to deploy
- Dependency management through **npm**
- There are hundreds of libraries to integrate with the majority of standard protocols

These reasons, along with others that we will develop in the following chapters, make Node.js the perfect candidate for building solid microservices.

API aggregation

Seneca is the framework that I have chosen for development in the following chapters. One of the most attractive characteristics of Seneca is API aggregation.

API aggregation is an advanced technique to compose an interface by aggregating different functionalities (plugins, methods, and so on) to it.

Let's take a look at the following example:

```
var express = require('express');
var app = express();

app.get('/sayhello', function (req, res) {
  res.send('Hello World!');
});
app.get('/saygoodbye', function(req, res) {
  res.send('Bye bye!');
});

var server = app.listen(3000, function () {
  var host = server.address().address;
  var port = server.address().port;
  console.log('App listening at http://%s:%s', host, port);
});
```

The preceding example uses Express, a very popular web framework for Node.js. This framework is also built around the API aggregation technique. Let's take a look at the fourth and seventh lines. In these lines, the developer registers two methods that are to be executed when someone hits the URLs /sayhello and /saygoodbye with a GET request. In other words, the application is composed of different smaller and independent implementations that are exposed to the outer world on a single interface, in this case, an app listening on the 3000 port.

In the following chapters, I will explain why this property is important and how to take advantage of it when building (and scaling) microservices.

The future of Node.js

JavaScript was first designed to be a language executed in the web browser. For those who worked or studied, using C/C++ was very familiar and that was the key for its adoption as a standard for the dynamic manipulation of documents in Web 2.0. **Asynchronous JavaScript and XML (AJAX)** was the detonator for JavaScript growth. Different browsers had different implementations of the request objects so that the developers had a hard time to write a cross-browser code.

The lack of standards led to the creation of many frameworks that encapsulated the logic behind AJAX, making easy-to-write cross-browser scripts.

JavaScript is a script language. It was not designed to be object oriented, neither was it designed to be the language of choice for large applications as the code tends to get chaotic and it is hard to enforce standards across different companies on how the code should be laid out. Every single company where I worked has different *best practices* and some of them are even contradictory.

European Computer Manufacturers Association (ECMA) came to the rescue. **ECMAScript 6**, the next standard for ECMA languages (JavaScript, ActionScript, Rhino, and so on) introduces the concept of classes, inheritance, collections, and a number of interesting features that will make the development of JavaScript software easier and more standard than the actual V8 specification.

One of these features that I consider more interesting is the introduction of the **class** keyword that allows us to model our JavaScript software with objects.

At the moment, the majority of browsers support a large number of these features, but when it comes to Node.js, only a few of them are implemented by default and some of them are implemented by passing special flags to the interpreter (harmony flags).

In this book, I will try to avoid the ECMAScript 6 features, sticking to the V8 specification as it is widely known by the majority of developers and, once someone knows JavaScript V8, it is fairly easy to ramp up on ECMAScript 6.

Summary

In this chapter, we studied the key concepts around microservices, as well as the best practices to be followed when designing high-quality software components towards building robust and resilient software architectures that enable us to respond quickly to the business needs.

You have also learned the key benefits such as the possibility of using the right language for the right service (technology heterogeneity) on the microservices-oriented architectures as well as some of the pitfalls that could make our life harder, such as the overhead on the operational side caused by the distributed nature of the microservices-oriented architectures.

Finally, we discussed why Node.js is a great tool for building microservices, as well as how we could benefit from JavaScript to build high-quality software components through techniques like API aggregation.

In the following chapters, we will be developing the concepts discussed in this chapter, with code examples and further explanation about the topics I have learned over the years.

As explained before, we will focus on the V8 version of JavaScript, but I will provide some hints on how to easily write upgradeable components to embrace ECMAScript 6.

2
Microservices in Node.js – Seneca and PM2 Alternatives

In this chapter, you will mainly learn about two frameworks, **Seneca** and **PM2**, and why they are important for building microservices. We will also get to know the alternatives to these frameworks in order to get a general understanding of what is going on in the Node.js ecosystem. In this chapter, we are going to focus on the following topics:

- **Need for Node.js**: In this section, we are going to justify the choice of Node.js as a framework to build our microservices-oriented software. We will walk through the software stack required to use this awesome technology.

- **Seneca – a microservices framework**: In this section, you will learn the basics of Seneca and why it is the right choice if we want to keep our software manageable. We will explain how to integrate Seneca with Express (the most popular web server in Node.js) in order to follow the industry standards.

- **PM2**: PM2 is the best choice to run Node.js applications. No matter what your problem in deploying your ecosystem of apps is, PM2 will always have a solution for it.

Need for Node.js

In the previous chapter, I mentioned that I wasn't a big fan of Node.js in the past. The reason for this was that I wasn't prepared to cope with the level of standardization that JavaScript was undergoing.

JavaScript in the browser was painful. Cross-browser compatibility was always a problem and the lack of standardization didn't help to ease the pain.

Then Node.js came and it was easy to create highly scalable applications due to its non-blocking nature (we will talk about it later in this chapter) and it was also very easy to learn as it was based on JavaScript, a well-known language.

Nowadays, Node.js is the preferred choice for a large number of companies across the world, as well as the number one choice for aspects that require a non-blocking nature in the server, such as web sockets.

In this book, we will primarily (but not only) use Seneca and PM2 as the frameworks for building and running microservices, but it does not mean that the alternatives are not good.

There are few alternatives in the market such as **restify** or **Express** for building applications and **forever** or **nodemon** to run them. However, I find Seneca and PM2 to be the most appropriate combination for building microservices for the following reasons:

- PM2 is extremely powerful regarding application deployments
- Seneca is not only a framework to build microservices, but it is also a paradigm that reshapes what we know about object-oriented software

We will be using Express in a few examples in the chapters of this book and we will also discuss how to integrate Seneca in Express as a middleware.

However, before that, let's discuss some concepts around Node.js that will help us to understand those frameworks.

Installing Node.js, npm, Seneca, and PM2

Node.js is fairly easy to install. Depending on your system, there is an installer available that makes the installation of Node.js and **npm** (**Node Package Manager**) a fairly simple task. Simply double-click on it and follow the instructions. At the time of writing this book, there are installers available for Windows and OSX.

However, the advanced users, especially DevOps engineers, will need to install Node.js and npm from the sources or binaries.

Both Node.js and npm programs come bundled together in a single package that we can download for various platforms from the Node.js website (either sources or binaries):

`https://nodejs.org/en/download/`

For the Chef users, a popular configuration management software to build servers, there are few options available, but the most popular is the following recipe (for those unfamiliar with Chef, a recipe is basically a script to install or configure software in a server through Chef):

`https://github.com/redguide/nodejs`

At the time of writing this book, there are binaries available for Linux.

Learning npm

npm is a software that comes with Node.js and enables you to pull dependencies from the Internet without worrying about their management. It can also be used to maintain and update dependencies, as well as create projects from scratch.

As you probably know, every node app comes with a `package.json` file. This file describes the configuration of the project (dependencies, versions, common commands, and so on). Let's see the following example:

```
{
    "name": "test-project",
    "version": "1.0.0",
    "description": "test project",
    "main": "index.js",
    "scripts": {
    "test": "grunt validate --verbose"
    },
    "author". "David Gonzalez",
    "license": "ISC"
}
```

The file itself is self-explanatory. There is an interesting section in the file—`scripts`.

In this section, we can specify the command that is used to run for different actions. In this case, if we run `npm test` from the terminal, npm will execute `grunt validate --verbose`.

Node applications are usually as easy to run as executing the following command:

`node index.js`

In the root of your project, consider that the bootstrapping file is index.js. If this is not the case, the best thing you can do is add a subsection in the scripts section in package.json, as follows:

```
"scripts": {
  "test": "grunt validate --verbose"
  "start": "node index.js"
},
```

As you can see, now we have two commands executing the same program:

node index.js

npm start

The benefits of using npm start are quite obvious—uniformity. No matter how complex your application is, npm start will always run it (if you have configured the scripts section correctly).

Let's install Seneca and PM2 on a clean project.

First, execute npm init in a new folder from the terminal after installing Node.js. You should get a prompt similar to the following image:

```
This utility will walk you through creating a package.json file.
It only covers the most common items, and tries to guess sane defaults.

See `npm help json` for definitive documentation on these fields
and exactly what they do.

Use `npm install <pkg> --save` afterwards to install a package and
save it as a dependency in the package.json file.

Press ^C at any time to quit.
name: (newfolder)
```

npm will ask you for a few parameters to configure your project, and once you are done, it writes a package.json file with content similar to the preceding code.

Now we need to install the dependencies; npm will do that for us. Just run the following command:

npm install --save seneca

Now, if you inspect `package.json` again, you can see that there is a new section called `dependencies` that contains an entry for Seneca:

```
"dependencies": {
  "seneca": "^0.7.1"
}
```

This means that from now on, our app can require the Seneca module and the `require()` function will be able to find it. There are a few variations of the `save` flag, as follows:

- `save`: This saves the dependency in the `dependencies` section. It is available through all the development life cycle.

- `save-dev`: This saves the dependency in the `devDependencies` section. It is only available in development and does not get deployed into production.

- `save-optional`: This adds a dependency (such as `save`), but lets npm continue if the dependency can't be found. It is up to the app to handle the lack of this dependency.

Let's continue with PM2. Although it can be used as a library, PM2 is mainly a command tool, like `ls` or `grep` in any Unix system. npm does a great job installing command-line tools:

```
npm install -g pm2
```

The `-g` flags instruct npm to globally install PM2, so it is available in the system, not in the app. This means that when the previous command finishes, `pm2` is available as a command in the console. If you run `pm2 help` in a terminal, you can see the help of PM2.

Our first program – Hello World

One of the most interesting concepts around Node.js is simplicity. You can learn Node.js in few days and master it in a few weeks, as long as you are familiar with JavaScript. Code in Node.js tends to be shorter and clearer than in other languages:

```
var http = require('http');

var server = http.createServer(function (request, response) {
  response.writeHead(200, {"Content-Type": "text/plain"});
  response.end("Hello World\n");
});

server.listen(8000);
```

The preceding code creates a server that listens on the 8000 port for requests. If you don't believe it, open a browser and type http://127.0.0.1:8000 in the navigation bar, as shown in the following screenshot:

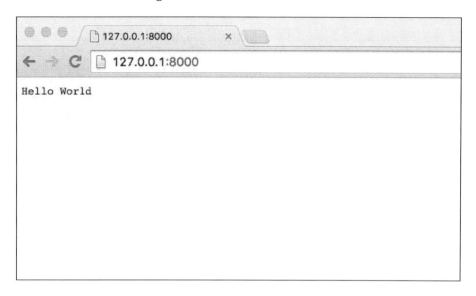

Let's explain the code:

- The first line loads the http module. Through the require() instruction, we ask the node to load the http module and assign the export of this module to the http variable. Exporting language elements is the way that Node.js has to expose functions and variables to the outer world from inside a module.

- The second construction in the script creates the HTTP server. The http module creates and exposes a method called createServer() that receives a function (remember JavaScript treats functions as first-level objects so that they can be passed as other functions arguments) as a parameter that, in the Node.js world, is called **callback**. A callback is an action to be executed as a response to an event. In this case, the event is that the script receives an HTTP request. Node.js has a heavy usage of callbacks due to its thread model. Your application will always be executed on a single thread so that not blocking the application thread while waiting for operations to complete and prevents our application from looking stalled or hanged. Otherwise, your program won't be responsive. We'll come back to this in *Chapter 4, Writing Your First Microservice in Node.js*.

- In the next line, server.listen(8000) starts the server. From now on, every time our server receives a request, the callback on the http.createServer() function will be executed.

This is it. Simplicity is the key to Node.js programs. The code allows you to go to the point without writing tons of classes, methods, and config objects that complicate what, in the first instance, can be done much more simply: write a script that serves requests.

Node.js threading model

Programs written in Node.js are single-threaded. The impact of this is quite significant; in the previous example, if we have ten thousand concurrent requests, they will be queued and satisfied by the Node.js event loop (it will be further explained in *Chapter 4*, *Writing Your First Microservice in Node.js* and *Chapter 6*, *Testing and Documenting Node.js Microservices*) one by one.

At first glance, this sounds wrong. I mean, the modern CPUs can handle multiple parallel requests due to their multicore nature. So, what is the benefit of executing them in one thread?

The answer to this question is that Node.js was designed to handle asynchronous processing. This means that in the event of a slow operation such as reading a file, instead of blocking the thread, Node.js allows the thread to continue satisfying other events, and then the control process of the node will execute the method associated with the event, processing the response.

Sticking to the previous example, the `createServer()` method accepts a callback that will be executed in the event of an HTTP request, but meanwhile, the thread is free to keep executing other actions.

The catch in this model is what Node.js developers call the callback hell. The code gets complicated as every single action that is a response to a blocking action has to be processed on a callback, like in the previous example; the function used as a parameter to the `createServer()` method is a good example.

Modular organization best practices

The source code organization for big projects is always controversial. Different developers have different approaches to how to order the source code in order to keep the chaos away.

Some languages such as Java or C# organize the code in packages so that we can find source code files that are related inside a package. As an example, if we are writing a task manager software, inside the `com.taskmanager.dao` package we can expect to find classes that implement the **data access object** (**DAO**) pattern in order to access the database. In the same way, in the `com.taskmanager.dao.domain.model` package, we can find all the classes that represent model objects (usually tables) in our application.

This is a convention in Java and C#. If you are a C# developer, and you start working on an existing project, it only takes you a few days to get used to how the code is structured as the language enforces the organization of the source.

Javascript

JavaScript was first designed to be run inside the browser. The code was supposed to be embedded in HTML documents so that the **Document Object Model (DOM)** could be manipulated to create dynamic effects. Take a look at the following example:

```html
<!DOCTYPE html>
<html>
<head>
  <meta charset="UTF-8">
  <title>Title of the document</title>
</head>
<body>
  Hello <span id="world">Mundo</span>
  <script type="text/javascript">
  document.getElementById("world").innerText = 'World';
  </script>
</body>
</html>
```

As you can see, if you load this HTML on a browser, the text inside the span tag with the id as world is replaced when the page loads.

In JavaScript, there is no concept of dependency management. JavaScript can be segregated from the HTML into its own file, but there is no way (for now) to include a JavaScript file into another JavaScript file.

This leads to a big problem. When the project contains dozens of JavaScript files, the assets management become more of an art than an engineering effort.

The order in which you import the JavaScript files becomes important as the browser executes the JavaScript files as it finds them. Let's reorder the code in the previous example to demonstrate it, as follows:

```html
<!DOCTYPE html>
<html>
<head>
  <meta charset="UTF-8">
  <title>Title of the document</title>
  <script type="text/javascript">
    document.getElementById("world").innerText = 'World';
  </script>
```

```
    </head>
    <body>
      Hello <span id="world">Mundo</span>

    </body>
    </html>
```

Now, save this HTML in an `index.html` file and try to load it in any browser, as shown in the following image:

In this case, I have used Chrome and the console shows an **Uncaught TypeError: Cannot set property 'innerText' of null** error in line 7.

Why is that happening?

As we explained earlier, the browser *executes* the code as it is found, and it turns out that when the browser executes the JavaScript, the `world` element does not exist yet.

Fortunately, Node.js has solved the dependency-loading problem using a very elegant and standard approach.

SOLID design principles

When talking about microservices, we always talk about modularity, and modularity always boils down to the following (**SOLID**) design principles:

- **Single** responsibility principle
- **Open** for extension, closed for modification
- **Liskov** substitution
- **Interface** segregation
- **Dependency** inversion (inversion of control and dependency injection)

You want your code to be organized in modules. A module is an aggregation of code that does something simple, such as manipulating strings, and it does it well. The more functions (or classes, utilities, and so on) your module contains, the less cohesive it is, and we are trying to avoid that.

In Node.js, every JavaScript file is a module by default. We can also use folders as modules, but let's focus on files:

```
function contains(a, b) {
  return a.indexOf(b) > -1;
}

function stringToOrdinal(str) {
  var result = ""
  for (var i = 0, len = str.length; i < len; i++) {
    result += charToNumber(str[i]);
  }
  return result;
}

function charToNumber(char) {
  return char.charCodeAt(0) - 96;
}

module.exports = {
  contains: contains,
  stringToOrdinal: stringToOrdinal
}
```

The preceding code represents a valid module in Node.js. In this case, the module contains three functions, where two of them are exposed to the outside of the module.

In Node.js, this is done through the `module.exports` variable. Whatever you assign to this variable is going to be visible by the calling code so that we can simulate private content on a module, such as the `charToNumber()` function in this case.

So, if we want to use this module, we just need to `require()` it, as follows:

```
var stringManipulation = require("./string-manipulation");
console.log(stringManipulation.stringToOrdinal("aabb"));
```

This should output 1122.

Let's go back to the SOLID principles and see how our module looks:

- **Single responsibility principle**: Our module only deals with strings
- **Open for extension, closed for modification**: We can add more functions, but the ones that we have are correct and they can be used to build new functions in the module
- **Liskov substitution**: We will skip this one, as the structure of the module is irrelevant to fulfil this principle
- **Interface segregation**: JavaScript is not a language that counts with an interface element such as Java or C#, but in this module, we exposed the interface, and the `module.exports` variable will act as a contract for the calling code and the change in our implementation won't affect how the module is being called
- **Dependency inversion**: Here is where we fail, not fully, but enough to reconsider our approach

In this case, we require the module, and the only way to interact with it is through the global scope. If, inside the module, we want to interact with data from outside, the only possible option is to create a global variable (or function) prior to requiring the module, and then assume that it is always going to be in there.

Global variables are a big problem in Node.js. As you are probably aware, in JavaScript, if you omit the `var` keyword when declaring a variable, it is automatically global.

This, coupled with the fact that intentional global variables create a data coupling between modules (coupling is what we want to avoid at any cost), is the reason to find a better approach to how to define the modules for our microservices (or in general).

Let's restructure the code as follows:

```
function init(options) {

  function charToNumber(char) {
    return char.charCodeAt(0) - 96;
  }

  function StringManipulation() {
  }

  var stringManipulation = new StringManipulation();

  stringManipulation.contains = function(a, b) {
```

```
      return a.indexOf(b) > -1;
    };

    stringManipulation.stringToOrdinal = function(str) {
      var result = ""
      for (var i = 0, len = str.length; i < len; i++) {
        result += charToNumber(str[i]);
      }
      return result;
    }
    return stringManipulation;
  }

  module.exports = init;
```

This looks a bit more complicated, but once you get used to it, the benefits are enormous:

- We can pass configuration parameters to the module (such as debugging information)
- Avoids the pollution of global scope as if everything is wrapped inside a function, and we enforce the *use strict* configuration (this avoids declarations without `var` with a compilation error)
- Parameterizing a module makes it easy to mock behaviors and data for testing

In this book, we are going to be writing a good amount of code to model systems from the microservices prospective. We will try to keep this pattern as much as we can so that we can see the benefits.

One of the library that we are going to be using to build microservices, Seneca, follows this pattern, as well as a large number of libraries that can be found on Internet.

Seneca – a microservices framework

Seneca is a framework for building microservices written by Richard Rodger, the founder and CTO of nearForm, a consultancy that helps other companies design and implement software using Node.js. Seneca is about simplicity, it connects services through a sophisticated pattern-matching interface that abstracts the transport from the code so that it is fairly easy to write highly scalable software.

Let's stop talking and see some examples:

```
var seneca = require( 'seneca' )()

seneca.add({role: 'math', cmd: 'sum'}, function (msg, respond) {
  var sum = msg.left + msg.right
  respond(null, {answer: sum})
})

seneca.add({role: 'math', cmd: 'product'}, function (msg, respond) {
  var product = msg.left * msg.right
  respond( null, { answer: product } )
})

seneca.act({role: 'math', cmd: 'sum', left: 1, right: 2},
  console.log)
    seneca.act({role: 'math', cmd: 'product', left: 3, right: 4},
  console.log)
```

As you can see, the code is self-explanatory:

- Seneca comes as a module, so the first thing that needs to be done is to `require()` it. Seneca package is wrapped in a function, so invoking the function initializes the library.

- Next two instructions are related to a concept explained in *Chapter 1, Microservices Architecture*: API composition. The `seneca.add()` method instructs Seneca to add a function that will be invoked with a set of patterns. For the first one, we specify an action that will take place when Seneca receives the {role: `math`, `cmd`: `sum`} command. For the second one, the pattern is {role: `math`, `cmd`: `product`}.

- The last line sends a command to Seneca that will be executed by the service that matches the pattern passed as the first parameter. In this case, it will match the first service as `role` and `cmd` match. The second call to act will match the second service.

Write the code in a file called `index.js` in the project that we created earlier in this chapter (remember that we installed Seneca and PM2), and run the following command:

```
node index.js
```

The output will be something similar to the following image:

```
→ code  node index.js
2016-03-07T20:28:20.636Z 3xdlpxcs8rjk/1457382500629/2233/- INFO hello    Seneca/1.3.0/3xdlpxcs8rjk/1457382500629/2233/-
null { answer: 3 }
null { answer: 12 }
```

We will talk about this output later in order to explain exactly what it means, but if you are used to enterprise applications, you can almost guess what is going on.

The last two lines are the responses from the two services: the first one executes `1+2` and the second one executes `3*4`.

The `null` output that shows up as the first word in the last two lines corresponds to a pattern that is widely used in JavaScript: the error first callback.

Let's explain it with a code example:

```javascript
var seneca = require( 'seneca' )()

seneca.add({role: 'math', cmd: 'sum'}, function (msg, respond) {
   var sum = msg.left + msg.right
   respond(null, {answer: sum})
})

seneca.add({role: 'math', cmd: 'product'}, function (msg, respond) {
   var product = msg.left * msg.right
   respond( null, { answer: product } )
})

seneca.act({role: 'math', cmd: 'sum', left: 1, right: 2},
   function(err, data) {
   if (err) {
     return console.error(err);
   }
   console.log(data);
});
seneca.act({role: 'math', cmd: 'product', left: 3, right: 4},
   console.log);
```

The previous code rewrites the first invocation to Seneca with a more appropriate approach. Instead of dumping everything into the console, process the response from Seneca, which is a callback where the first parameter is the error, if one happened (`null` otherwise), and the second parameter is the data coming back from the microservice. This is why, in the first example, `null` was the first output into the console.

In the world of Node.js, it is very common to use callbacks. Callbacks are a way of indicating to the program that something has happened, without being blocked until the result is ready to be processed. Seneca is not an exception to this. It relies heavily on callbacks to process the response to service calls, which makes more sense when you think about microservices being deployed in different machines (in the previous example, everything runs in the same machine), especially because the network latency can be something to factor into the design of your software.

Inversion of control done right

Inversion of control is a must in modern software. It comes together with the dependency injection.

Inversion of control can be defined as *a technique to delegate the creation or call of components and methods so that your module does not need to know how to build the dependencies, which usually, are obtained through the dependency injection.*

Seneca does not really make use of the dependency injection, but it is the perfect example of inversion of control.

Let's take a look at the following code:

```
var seneca = require('seneca')();
seneca.add({component: 'greeter'}, function(msg, respond) {
  respond(null, {message: 'Hello ' + msg.name});
});
seneca.act({component: 'greeter', name: 'David'}, function(error,
  response) {
  if(error) return console.log(error);
  console.log(response.message);
});
```

This is the most basic Seneca example. From enterprise software's point of view, we can differentiate two components here: a producer (Seneca.add()) and a consumer (Seneca.act()). As mentioned earlier, Seneca does not have a dependency injection system as is, but Seneca is gracefully built around the inversion of control principle.

In the Seneca.act() function, we don't explicitly call the component that holds the business logic; instead of that, we ask Seneca to resolve the component for us through the use of an interface, in this case, a JSON message. This is inversion of control.

Seneca is quite flexible around it: no keywords (except for integrations) and no mandatory fields. It just has a combination of keywords and values that are used by a pattern matching engine called **Patrun**.

Pattern matching in Seneca

Pattern matching is one of the most flexible software patterns that you can use for microservices.

As opposed to network addresses or messages, patterns are fairly easy to extend. Let's explain it with the help of the following example:

```
var seneca = require('seneca')();
seneca.add({cmd: 'wordcount'}, function(msg, respond) {
  var length = msg.phrase.split(' ').length;
  respond(null, {words: length});
});

seneca.act({cmd: 'wordcount', phrase: 'Hello world this is
  Seneca'}, function(err, response) {
  console.log(response);
});
```

It is a service that counts the number of words in a sentence. As we have seen before, in the first line, we add the handler for the wordcount command, and in the second one, we send a request to Seneca to count the number of words in a phrase.

If you execute it, you should get something similar to the following image:

```
→ code  node string-require.js
1122
```

By now, you should be able to understand how it works and even make some modifications to it.

Let's extend the pattern. Now, we want to skip the short words, as follows:

```
var seneca = require('seneca')();

seneca.add({cmd: 'wordcount'}, function(msg, respond) {
  var length = msg.phrase.split(' ').length;
  respond(null, {words: length});
});

seneca.add({cmd: 'wordcount', skipShort: true}, function(msg,
  respond) {
  var words = msg.phrase.split(' ');
  var validWords = 0;
  for (var i = 0; i < words.length; i++) {
```

```
      if (words[i].length > 3) {
        validWords++;
      }
    }
    respond(null, {words: validWords});
});

seneca.act({cmd: 'wordcount', phrase: 'Hello world this is
  Seneca'}, function(err, response) {
  console.log(response);
});

seneca.act({cmd: 'wordcount', skipShort: true, phrase: 'Hello
  world this is Seneca'}, function(err, response) {
  console.log(response);
});
```

As you can see, we have added another handler for the wordcount command with an extra skipShort parameter.

This handler now skips all the words with three or fewer characters. If you execute the preceding code, the output is similar to the following image:

```
➜  code  node wordcount.js
2015-11-01T13:50:05.889Z hrzpzs2mgt2n/1446385805876/3897/- INFO hello    Seneca/0.7.2/hrzpzs2mgt2n/1446385805876/3897/-
{ words: 5 }
{ words: 4 }
```

The first line, {words: 5}, corresponds to the first act call. The second line, {words: 4}, corresponds to the second call.

Patrun – a pattern-matching library

Patrun is also written by Richard Rodger. It is used by Seneca in order to execute the pattern matching and decide which service should respond to the call.

Patrun uses a **closest match** approach to resolve the calls. Let's see the following example:

```
{ x:1,      } -> A
{ x:1, y:1 } -> B
{ x:1, y:2 } -> C
```

In the preceding image, we can see three patterns. These are equivalent to seneca. add() from the example in the previous section.

In this case, we are registering three different combinations of *x* and *y* variables. Now, let's see how Patrun does the matching:

- {x: 1} ->A: This matches 100% with **A**
- {x: 2} ->: No match
- {x:1, y:1} -> B: 100% match with **B**; it also matches with **A**, but **B** is a better match—two out of two vs one out of one
- {x:1, y:2} -> C: 100% match with **C**; again, it also matches with **A**, but **C** is more concrete
- {y: 1} ->: No match

As you can see, Patrun (and Seneca) will always get the longest match. In this way, we can easily extend the functionality of the more abstract patterns by concreting the matching.

Reusing patterns

In the preceding example, in order to skip the words with fewer than three characters, we don't reuse the word count function.

In this case, it is quite hard to reuse the function as is; although the problem sounds very similar, the solution barely overlaps.

However, let's go back to the example where we add two numbers:

```
var seneca = require( 'seneca' )()

seneca.add({role: 'math', cmd: 'sum'}, function (msg, respond) {
  var sum = msg.left + msg.right
  respond(null, {answer: sum})
});

seneca.add({role: 'math', cmd: 'sum', integer: true}, function
  (msg, respond) {
  this.act({role: 'math', cmd: 'sum', left: Math.floor(msg.left),
    right: Math.floor(msg.right) },respond);
});

seneca.act({role: 'math', cmd: 'sum', left: 1.5, right: 2.5},
  console.log)

seneca.act({role: 'math', cmd: 'sum', left: 1.5, right: 2.5,
  integer: true}, console.log)
```

As you can see, the code has changed a bit. Now, the pattern that accepts an integer relies on the base pattern to calculate the sum of the numbers.

Patrun always tries to match the closest and most concrete pattern that it can find with the following two dimensions:

- The longest chain of matches
- The order of the patterns

It will always try to find the best fit, and if there is an ambiguity, it will match the first pattern found.

In this way, we can rely on already-existing patterns to build new services.

Writing plugins

Plugins are an important part of applications based on Seneca. As we discussed in *Chapter 1, Microservices Architecture*, the API aggregation is the perfect way of building applications.

Node.js' most popular frameworks are built around this concept: small pieces of software that are combined to create a bigger system.

Seneca is also built around this; Seneca.add() principle adds a new piece to the puzzle so that the final API is a mixture of different small software pieces.

Seneca goes one step further and implements an interesting plugin system so that the common functionality can be modularized and abstracted into reusable components.

The following example is the minimal Seneca plugin:

```
function minimal_plugin( options ) {
  console.log(options)
}

require( 'seneca' )()
  .use( minimal_plugin, {foo:'bar'} )
```

Write the code into a minimal-plugin.js file and execute it:

```
node minimal-plugin.js
```

The output of this execution should be something similar to the following image:

```
→ code node minimal-plugin.js
2016-04-10T22:22:14.849Z lojwswfluxej/1460326934841/6893/- INFO hello    Seneca/1
.3.0/lojwswfluxej/1460326934841/6893/-
{ foo: 'bar' }
```

In Seneca, a plugin is loaded at the startup, but we don't see it as the default log level is INFO. This means that Seneca won't show any DEBUG level info. In order to see what Seneca is doing, we need to get more information, as follows:

```
node minimal-plugin.js –seneca.log.all
```

This produces a huge output. This is pretty much everything that is happening inside Seneca, which can be very useful to debug complicated situations, but in this case, what we want to do is show a list of plugins:

```
node minimal-plugin.js --seneca.log.all | grep plugin | grep DEFINE
```

It will produce something similar to the following image:

```
2015-11-01T20:43:38.969Z 5kptab6ee6b4/1466410618929/4276/- DEBUG  plugin  basic          DEFINE  {}
2015-11-01T20:43:39.230Z 5kptab6ee6b4/1466410618929/4276/- DEBUG  plugin  transport DEFINE  {}
2015-11-01T20:43:39.388Z 5kptab6ee6b4/1466410618929/4276/- DEBUG  plugin  web            DEFINE  {}
2015-11-01T20:43:39.420Z 5kptab6ee6b4/1466410618929/4276/- DEBUG  plugin  mem-store DEFINE  {}
2015-11-01T20:43:39.425Z 5kptab6ee6b4/1466410618929/4276/- DEBUG  plugin  minimal_plugin DEFINE  {foo:bar}
```

Let's analyze the preceding output:

- `basic`: This plugin is included with the main Seneca module and provides a small set of basic utility action patterns.

- `transport`: This is the transport plugin. Up until now, we have only executed different services (quite small and concise) on the same machine, but what if we want to distribute them? This plugin will help us with that, and we will see how to do so in the following sections.

- `web`: In *Chapter 1, Microservices Architecture*, we mentioned that the microservices should advocate to keep the pipes that connect them under a standard that is widely used. Seneca uses TCP by default, but creating a RESTful API can be tricky. This plugin helps to do it, and we will see how to do this in the following section.

- `mem-store`: Seneca comes with a data abstraction layer so that we can handle the data storage in different places: Mongo, SQL databases, and so on. Out of the box, Seneca provides an in-memory storage so that it just works.

- `minimal_plugin`: This is our plugin. So, now we know that Seneca is able to load it.

The plugin we wrote does nothing. Now, it is time to write something useful:

```
function math( options ) {

  this.add({role:'math', cmd: 'sum'}, function( msg, respond ) {
    respond( null, { answer: msg.left + msg.right } )
```

```
  })

  this.add({role:'math', cmd: 'product'}, function( msg, respond )
    {
    respond( null, { answer: msg.left * msg.right } )
  })

}

require( 'seneca' )()
  .use( math )
  .act( 'role:math,cmd:sum,left:1,right:2', console.log )
```

First of all, notice that in the last instruction, `act()` follows a different format. Instead of passing a dictionary, we pass a string with the same key values as the first argument, as we did with a dictionary. There is nothing wrong with it, but my preferred approach is to use the JSON objects (dictionaries), as it is a way of structuring the data without having syntax problems.

In the previous example, we can see how the code got structured as a plugin. If we execute it, we can see that the output is similar to the following one:

```
→ code  node math.js
2016-03-07T20:39:33.145Z kw4uoq06n1xg/1457383173137/2623/- INFO hello   Seneca/1.3.0/kw4uoq06n1xg/1457383173137/2623/-
null { answer: 3 }
```

One of the things you need to be careful about in Seneca is how to initialize your plugins. The function that wraps the plugin (in the preceding example, the `math()` function) is executed synchronously by design and it is called the **definition function**. If you remember from the previous chapter, Node.js apps are single-threaded.

To initialize a plugin, you add a special `init()` action pattern. This action pattern is called in sequence for each plugin. The `init()` function must call its respond callback without errors. If the plugin initialization fails, then Seneca exits the Node.js process. You want your microservices to fail fast (and scream loudly) when there's a problem. All plugins must complete initialization before any actions are executed.

Let's see an example of how to initialize a plugin in the following way:

```
function init(msg, respond) {
  console.log("plugin initialized!");
  console.log("expensive operation taking place now... DONE!");
  respond();
}

function math( options ) {

  this.add({role:'math', cmd: 'sum'}, function( msg, respond ) {
    respond( null, { answer: msg.left + msg.right } )
  })

  this.add({role:'math', cmd: 'product'}, function( msg, respond )
    {
    respond( null, { answer: msg.left * msg.right } )
  })

  this.add({init: "math"}, init);
}
require( 'seneca' )()
  .use( math )
  .act( 'role:math,cmd:sum,left:1,right:2', console.log )
```

Then, after executing this file, the output should look very similar to the following image:

```
➡ code  node expensive.js
2016-03-07T20:40:25.351Z bv8phjhz4b92/1457383225343/2640/- INFO hello  Seneca/1.3.0/bv8phjhz4b92/1457383225343/2640/-
plugin initialized!
expensive operation taking place now... DONE!
null { answer: 3 }
```

As you can read from the output, the function that initializes the plugin was called.

> The general rule in Node.js apps is to never block the thread. If you find yourself blocking the thread, you might need to rethink how to avoid it.

Web server integration

In *Chapter 1, Microservices Architecture*, we put a special emphasis on using standard technologies to communicate with your microservices.

Seneca, by default, uses a TCP transport layer that, although it uses TCP, is not easy to interact with, as the criteria to decide the method that gets executed is based on a payload sent from the client.

Let's dive into the most common use case: your service is called by JavaScript on a browser. Although it can be done, it would be much easier if Seneca exposed a REST API instead of the JSON dialog, which is perfect for communication between microservices (unless you have ultra-low latency requirements).

Seneca is not a web framework. It can be defined as a *general purpose microservices framework*, so it would not make too much sense to build it around a concrete case like the one exposed before.

Instead of that, Seneca was built in a way that makes the integration with other frameworks fairly easy.

Express is the first option when building web applications on Node.js. The amount of examples and documentation that can be found on Internet about Express makes the task of learning it fairly easy.

Seneca as Express middleware

Express was also built under the principle of API composition. Every piece of software in Express is called middleware, and they are chained in the code in order to process every request.

In this case, we are going to use **seneca-web** as a middleware for Express so that once we specify the configuration, all the URLs will follow a naming convention.

Let's consider the following example:

```
var seneca = require('seneca')()

seneca.add('role:api,cmd:bazinga',function(args,done){
  done(null,{bar:"Bazinga!"});
});
seneca.act('role:web',{use:{
  prefix: '/my-api',
  pin: {role:'api',cmd:'*'},

  map:{
    bazinga: {GET: true}
```

```
    }
}})
var express = require('express')
var app = express()
app.use( seneca.export('web') )
app.listen(3000)
```

This code is not as easy to understand as the previous examples, but I'll do my best to explain it:

- The second line adds a pattern to Seneca. We are pretty familiar with it as all the examples on this book do that.

- The third instruction, seneca.act(), is where the magic happens. We are mounting the patterns with the role:api pattern and any cmd pattern (cmd:*) to react to URLs under /my-api. In this example, the first seneca.add() will reply to the URL /my-api/bazinga, as /my-api/ is specified by the prefix variable and bazinga by the cmd part of the seneca.add() command.

- app.use(seneca.export('web')) instructs Express to use seneca-web as middleware to execute actions based on the configuration rules.

- app.listen(3000) binds the port 3000 to Express.

If you remember from an earlier section in this chapter, seneca.act() takes a function as a second parameter. In this case, we are exposing configuration to be used by Express on how to map the incoming requests to Seneca actions.

Let's test it:

The preceding code is pretty dense, so let's explain it down to the code from the browser:

- Express receives a request that is handled by seneca-web.

- The seneca-web plugin was configured to use /my-api/ as a prefix, which is being bound with the keyword `pin` (refer to `seneca.act()` from the preceding code) to Seneca actions (`seneca.add()`) that contain the `role:api` pattern, plus any cmd pattern (`cmd:*`). In this case, /my-api/bazinga corresponds to the first (and only) `seneca.add()` command with the `{role: 'api', cmd: 'bazinga'}` pattern.

It takes a while to fully understand the integration between Seneca and Express, but once it is clear, the flexibility offered by the API composability pattern is limitless.

Express itself is big enough to be out of the scope of this book, but it is worth taking a look as it is a very popular framework.

Data storage

Seneca comes with a data-abstraction layer that allows you to interact with the data of your application in a generic way.

By default, Seneca comes with an in-memory plugin (as explained in the previous section), therefore, it works out of the box.

We are going to be using it for the majority of this book, as the different storage systems are completely out of scope and Seneca abstracts us from them.

Seneca provides a simple data abstraction layer (**Object-relational mapping (ORM)**) based on the following operations:

- **load**: This loads an entity by identifier
- **save**: This creates or updates (if you provide an identifier) an entity
- **list**: This lists entities matching a simple query
- **remove**: This deletes an entity by an identifier

Let's build a plugin that manages employees in the database:

```
module.exports = function(options) {
  this.add({role: 'employee', cmd: 'add'}, function(msg, respond){
    this.make('employee').data$(msg.data).save$(respond);
  });

  this.find({role: 'employee', cmd: 'get'}, function(msg, respond)
    {
    this.make('employee').load$(msg.id, respond);
  });
}
```

Remember that the database is, by default, in memory, so we don't need to worry about the table structure for now.

The first command adds an employee to the database. The second command recovers an employee from the database by id.

Note that all the ORM primitives in Seneca end up with the dollar symbol ($).

As you can see now, we have been abstracted from the data storage details. If the application changes in the future and we decide to use MongoDB as a data storage instead of an in-memory storage, the only thing we need to take care of is the plugin that deals with MongoDB.

Let's use our employee management plugin, as shown in the following code:

```
var seneca = require('seneca')().use('employees-storage')
var employee = {
  name: "David",
  surname: "Gonzalez",
  position: "Software Developer"
}

function add_employee() {
  seneca.act({role: 'employee', cmd: 'add', data: employee},
    function (err, msg) {
    console.log(msg);
  });
}
add_employee();
```

In the preceding example, we add an employee to the in-memory database by invoking the pattern exposed in the plugin.

Along the book, we will see different examples about how to use the data abstraction layer, but the main focus will be on how to build microservices and not how to deal with the different data storages.

PM2 – a task runner for Node.js

PM2 is a production-process manager that helps to scale the Node.js up or down, as well as load balance the instances of the server. It also ensures that the processes are running constantly, tackling down one of the side effects of the thread model of Node.js: an uncaught exception kills the thread, which in turn kills your application.

Single-threaded applications and exceptions

As you learned before, Node.js applications are run in a single thread. This doesn't mean that Node.js is not concurrent, it only means that your application runs on a single thread, but everything else runs parallel.

This has an implication: *if an exception bubbles out without being handled, your application dies.*

The solution for this is making an intensive use of promises libraries such as **bluebird**; it adds handlers for success and failures so that if there is an error, the exception does not bubble out, killing your app.

However, there are some situations that we can't control, *we call them unrecoverable errors or bugs.* Eventually, your application will die due to a badly handled error. In languages such as Java, an exception is not a huge deal: the thread dies, but the application continues working.

In Node.js, it is a big problem. This problem was solved in the first instance using task runners such as **forever**.

Both of them are task runners that, when your application exits for some reason, rerun it again so it ensures the uptime.

Consider the following example:

```
➜  ~  forever helloWorld.js
warn:    --minUptime not set. Defaulting to: 1000ms
warn:    --spinSleepTime not set. Your script will exit if it does not stay up for at least 1000ms
Server running at http://127.0.0.1:8000/
```

The `helloWorld.js` application is now handled by forever, which will rerun it if the application dies. Let's kill it, as shown in the following image:

```
4902 ttys000    0:00.33 node /usr/local/bin/forever helloWorld.js
4903 ttys000    0:00.08 /usr/local/bin/node /Users/dgonzalez/helloWorld.js
```

As you can see, forever has spawned a different process with the 4903 PID. Now, we issue a kill command (`kill -9 4093`) and that is the output from forever, as follows:

```
→ ~  forever helloWorld.js
warn:    --minUptime not set. Defaulting to: 1000ms
warn:    --spinSleepTime not set. Your script will exit if it does not stay up for at least 1000ms
Server running at http://127.0.0.1:8000/
error: Forever detected script was killed by signal: SIGKILL
error: Script restart attempt #1
Server running at http://127.0.0.1:8000/
```

Although we have killed it, our application was respawned by forever without any downtime (at least, noticeable downtime).

As you can see, forever is pretty basic: it reruns the application as many times as it gets killed.

There is another package called **nodemon**, which is one of the most useful tools for developing Node.js applications. It reloads the application if it detects changes in the files that it monitors (by default, `*.*`):

```
→ ~  nodemon helloWorld.js
2 Nov 00:55:14 - [nodemon] v1.4.1
2 Nov 00:55:14 - [nodemon] to restart at any time, enter `rs`
2 Nov 00:55:14 - [nodemon] watching: *.*
2 Nov 00:55:14 - [nodemon] starting `node helloWorld.js`
Server running at http://127.0.0.1:8000/
```

Now, if we modify the `helloWorld.js` file, we can see how nodemon reloads the application. This is very interesting in order to avoid the edit/reload cycle and speed up the development.

Using PM2 – the industry-standard task runner

Although, forever looks very interesting, PM2 is a more advanced task runner than forever. With PM2, you can completely manage your application life cycle without any downtime, as well as scale your application up or down with a simple command.

PM2 also acts as a load balancer.

Let's consider the following example:

```
var http = require('http');

var server = http.createServer(function (request, response) {
  console.log('called!');
  response.writeHead(200, {"Content-Type": "text/plain"});
  response.end("Hello World\n");
});
server.listen(8000);
console.log("Server running at http://127.0.0.1:8000/");
```

This is a fairly simple application. Let's run it using PM2:

pm2 start helloWorld.js

This produces an output similar to the following image:

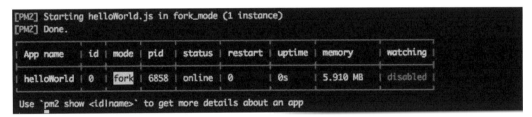

PM2 has registered an app named helloWorld. This app is running in the fork mode (that means, PM2 is not acting as a load balancer, it has just forked the app) and the PID of the operating system is 6858.

Now, as the following screen suggests, we will run pm2 show 0, which shows the information relevant to the app with id 0, as shown in the following image:

With two commands, we have managed to run a simple application in a very sophisticated way.

From now on, PM2 will ensure that your app is always running so that if your application dies, PM2 will restart it again.

We can also monitor the number of apps PM2 is running:

```
pm2 monit
```

This shows the following output:

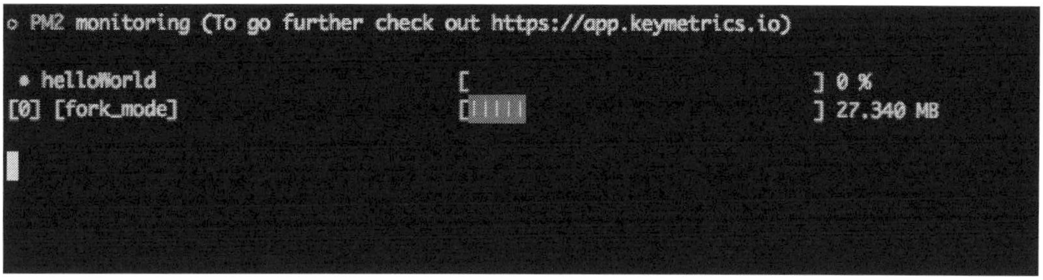

This is the PM2 monitor. In this case, it is a complete overkill as our system is only composed of one application, which runs in the fork mode.

We can also see the logs executing `pm2 logs` as shown in the following image:

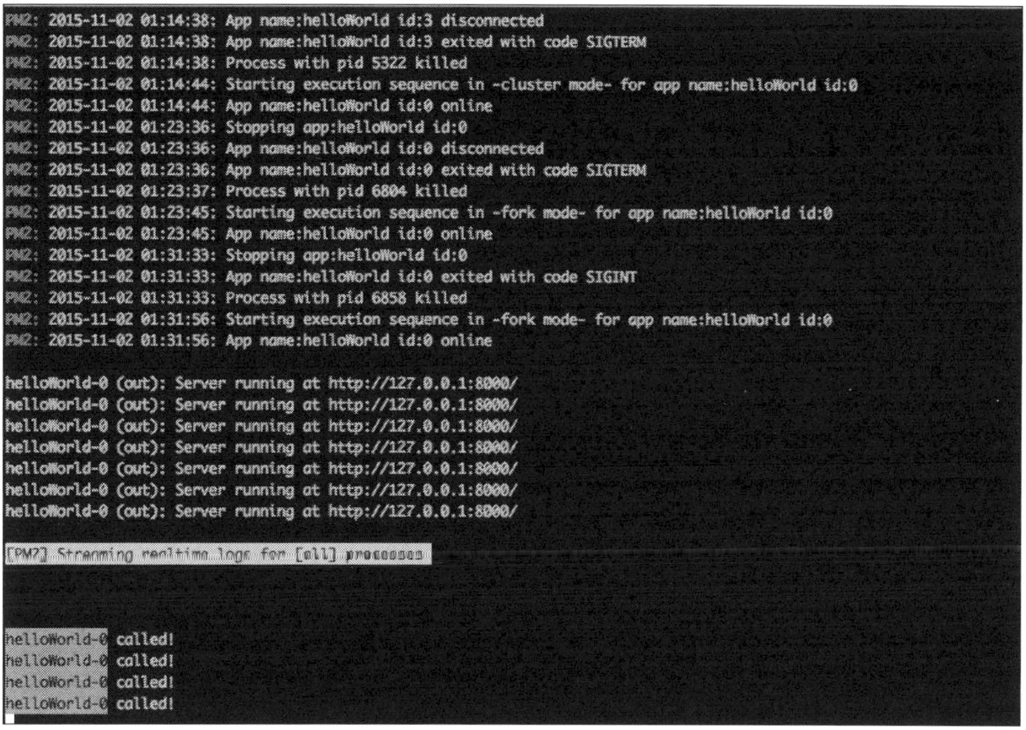

As you can see, PM2 feels solid. With few commands, we have covered 90% of the monitoring necessities of our application. However, this is not everything.

PM2 also comes with an easy way to reload your applications without downtime:

```
pm2 reload all
```

This command ensures that your apps are restarted with zero downtime. PM2 will queue the incoming requests for you and reprocess them once your app is responsive again. There is a more fine-grained option where you can specify reloading only certain apps by specifying the app name:

```
pm2 reload helloWorld
```

For those who have been fighting for years with Apache, NGINX, PHP-FPM, and so on, this will sound very familiar.

Another interesting feature in PM2 is running your application in the cluster mode. In this mode, PM2 spawns a controller process and as many workers (your app) as you specify so that you can take the benefit of multicore CPUs with a single-thread technology such as Node.js.

Before doing this, we need to stop our running application:

```
pm2 stop all
```

This will result in the following output:

App name	id	mode	pid	status	restart	uptime	memory	watching
helloWorld	0	fork	0	stopped	0	0	0 B	disabled

Use `pm2 show <id|name>` to get more details about an app

PM2 remembers the apps that were running, so before rerunning the app in the cluster mode, we need to inform PM2 to forget about your app, as follows:

```
pm2 delete all
```

```
[PM2] Deleting all process
[PM2] deleteProcessId process id 0
```

App name	id	mode	pid	status	restart	uptime	memory	watching

Use `pm2 show <id|name>` to get more details about an app

We are ready to run our app in the cluster mode:

```
pm2 start helloWorld.js -i 3
```

```
[PM2] Starting helloWorld.js in cluster_mode (3 instances)
[PM2] Done.

| App name     | id | mode    | pid  | status | restart | uptime | memory    | watching |
| helloWorld   | 0  | cluster | 7477 | online | 0       | 0s     | 26.023 MB | disabled |
| helloWorld   | 1  | cluster | 7478 | online | 0       | 0s     | 26.316 MB | disabled |
| helloWorld   | 2  | cluster | 7479 | online | 0       | 0s     | 24.203 MB | disabled |

Use `pm2 show <id|name>` to get more details about an app
```

PM2 is acting as a round-robin between the main process and the three workers so that they can cope with three requests at the same time. We can also scale down or up our number of workers:

```
pm2 scale helloWorld 2
```

This will result in two processes being run for the same app instead of three:

```
o PM2 monitoring (To go further check out https://app.keymetrics.io)

 • helloWorld             [              ] 0 %
 [1] [cluster_mode]       [||||||        ] 30.133 MB

 • helloWorld             [              ] 0 %
 [2] [cluster_mode]       [||||||        ] 30.477 MB
```

As you can see, with very little effort, we have managed to configure our app in order to be production ready.

Now, we can save the status of PM2 so that if we restart the server, and PM2 is running as a daemon, the apps will automatically start.

PM2 has a code API so that we can write a Node.js program to manage all the steps that we have been manually doing. It also has a way of configuring your services with a JSON file. We will discuss this in more depth in *Chapter 6, Testing and Documenting Node.js Microservices*, when we study how to use PM2 and Docker to deploy Node.js applications.

Summary

In this chapter, you learned the basics of Seneca and PM2 so that we will be able to build and run a microservices-oriented system in *Chapter 4, Writing Your First Microservice in Node.js,* of this book.

We have also demonstrated that a few of the concepts exposed in the previous chapter are actually helpful in solving real-world problems as well as making our life very easy.

In the next chapter, we will talk about how to split a monolithic application, a task for which we will need to know a few of the concepts developed during this chapter.

3
From the Monolith to Microservices

In my professional life, I have worked in quite a few different companies, mainly in financial services, and all of the companies that I have worked for follow the same pattern as shown in the following:

1. A company is set up by a couple of people with good domain knowledge: insurance, payments, credit cards, and so on.

2. The company grows, demanding new business requirements that need to be satisfied quickly (regulation, big customers demanding silly things, and so on), which are built in a hurry with little to no planning.

3. The company experiences another phase of growing, where the business transactions are clearly defined and poorly modelled by a hard-to-maintain monolithic software.

4. The company increases the headcount that drives into growing pains and loss of efficiency due to restrictions imposed on how the software was built in the first instance.

This chapter is not only about how to avoid the previous flow (uncontrolled organic growth), but it is also about how to model a new system using microservices. This chapter is the soul of this book, as I will try to synthetize my experience in a few pages, setting up the principles to be followed in *Chapter 4*, *Writing Your First Microservice in Node.js*, where we will be building a full system based on microservices using the lessons learned in the previous chapters.

First, there was the monolith

A huge percentage (my estimate is around 90%) of the modern enterprise software is built following a monolithic approach.

Large software components that run in a single container and have a well-defined development life cycle, which goes completely against the agile principles, deliver early and deliver often (`https://en.wikipedia.org/wiki/Release_early,_ release_often`), as follows:

- **Deliver early**: The sooner you fail, the easier it is to recover. If you are working for two years on a software component and then it is released, there is a huge risk of deviation from the original requirements, which are usually wrong and change every few days.

- **Deliver often**: Delivering often, the stakeholders are aware of the progress and can see the changes reflected quickly in the software. Errors can be fixed in a few days and improvements are identified easily.

Companies build big software components instead of smaller ones that work together as it is the natural thing to do, as shown in the following:

1. The developer has a new requirement.
2. He builds a new method on an existing class on the service layer.
3. The method is exposed on the API via HTTP, SOAP, or any other protocol.

Now, multiply it by the number of developers in your company, and you will obtain something called **organic growth**. Organic growth is a type of *uncontrolled and unplanned* growth on software systems under business pressure without an adequate long-term planning, and it is bad.

How to tackle organic growth?

The first thing required to tackle organic growth is to make sure that the business and IT are aligned in the company. Usually, in big companies, IT is not seen as a core part of the business.

Organizations outsource their IT systems, keeping the price in mind, but not the quality so that the partners building these software components are focused on one thing: *deliver on time* and according to the specifications even if they are incorrect.

This produces a less-than-ideal ecosystem to respond to the business needs with a working solution for an existing problem. IT is lead by people who barely understand how the systems are built, and usually overlook the complexity of software development.

Fortunately, this is a changing tendency as IT systems become the driver of 99% of the businesses around the world, but we need to get smarter about how we build them.

The first measure to tackle organic growth is aligning IT and business stakeholders to work together: educating the nontechnical stakeholders is the key to success.

If we go back to the few big releases schema. Can we do it better?

Of course we can. Divide the work into manageable software artifacts that model a single, well-defined business activity and give it an entity.

It does not need to be a microservice at this stage, but keeping the logic inside of a separated, well-defined, easily testable, and decoupled module will give us a huge advantage for future changes in the application.

Let's consider the following example:

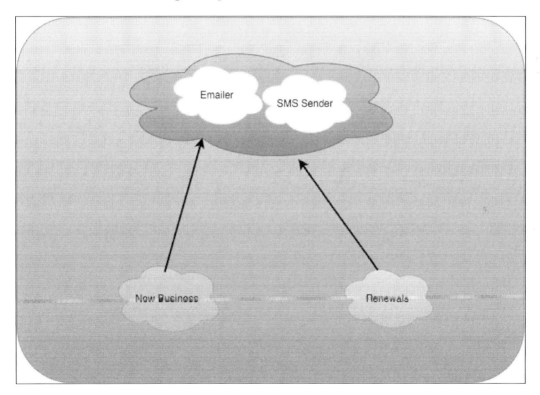

In this insurance system, you can see that someone was in a hurry. SMS and e-mail sender, although both are communication channels, they have a very different nature and you probably want them to act in different ways.

The calling services are grouped into the following two high-level entities:

- **New Business**: The new customers that receive an e-mail when they sign up
- **Renewals**: The existing customers that receive an SMS when the insurance policy is ready to be renewed

At some point, the system needed to send SMSs and e-mails and someone created the communication service entity that handles all the third-party communications.

It looks like a good idea in the beginning. SMS or e-mail, at the end of the day, is only a channel, the communication mechanism will be 90% same and we can reuse plenty of functionality.

What happens if we suddenly want to integrate a third-party service that handles all the physical post?

What happens if we want to add a newsletter that goes out to the customers once a week with information that we consider interesting for our customers?

The service will grow out of control and it will become more difficult to test, release, and ensure that the changes in the SMS code won't affect sending the e-mail in any form.

This is organic growth and, in this case, it is related to a law called **Conway's Law**, which states the following:

> *Any organization that designs a system (defined more broadly here than just information systems) will inevitably produce a design whose structure is a copy of the organization's communication structure.*

In this case, we are falling into a trap. We are trying to model the communication on a single software component that is probably too big and complex to react quickly to new business needs.

Let's take a look at the following diagram:

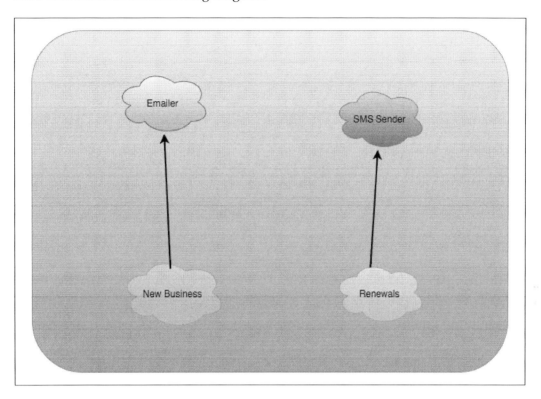

Now, we have encapsulated every communication channel on its own service (which, later on, will be deployed as a microservice) and we will do the same for future communication channels.

This is the first step to beat organic growth: create fine-grained services with well-defined boundaries and a single responsibility — *do something small, but do it well.*

How abstract is too abstract?

Our brain can't handle complicated mechanisms. The abstraction capacity is one of the most recent human intelligence acquisitions.

In the example from the previous section, I've given something for good, which will upset half of the programmers in the world: *eradicating the abstraction of our system.*

The abstraction capacity is something that we learn along the years and, unlike intelligence, it can be trained. Not everyone can reach the same level of abstraction, and if we mix the specific and complex domain knowledge required by some industries with a high-level of abstraction, we have the perfect recipe for a disaster.

When building software, one of the golden rules that I always tried to follow (and try is the correct word, as I always find huge opposition to it) is to avoid premature abstraction.

How many times did you find yourself in a corner with a simple set of requirements: *build a program to solve X*. However, your team goes off and anticipates all the possible variations of X, without even knowing if they are plausible. Then, once the software is in production, one of the stakeholders comes with a variation of X that you could have never imagined (as the requirements were not even correct) and now, getting this variation to work will cost you a few days and a massive refactor.

The way to avoid this problem is simple: *avoid abstraction without at least three use cases.*

Do not factor in the possibility of sending the data through different types of channels as it might not happen and you are compromising the current feature with unnecessary abstractions. Once you have at least one other communication channel, it is time to start thinking about how these two software components can be designed better, and when the third use case shows up, refactor.

Remember that when building microservices, they should be small enough to be rewritten on a single sprint (around two weeks), so the benefits of having a working prototype in such a short period of time is worth the risk of having to rewrite it once the requirements are more concrete: something to show to the stakeholders is the quickest way to nail down the requirements.

Seneca is great in this regard as, through pattern matching, we can extend the API of a given microservice without affecting the existing calling code: our service is open for extension, but closed for modification (the SOLID principles) as we are adding functionality without affecting the existing one. We will see more complete examples of this behavior in *Chapter 4, Writing Your First Microservice in Node.js*.

Then the microservices appeared

Microservices are here to stay. Nowadays, the companies give more importance to the quality of the software. As stated in the previous section, deliver early and deliver often are the key to succeed in software development.

Microservices are helping us to satisfy business needs as quickly as possible through modularity and specialization. Small pieces of software that can easily be versioned and upgraded within a few days and they are easy to test as they have a clear and small purpose (specialization) and are written in such a way that they are isolated from the rest of the system (modularization).

Unfortunately, it is not common to find the situation as described previously. Usually, big software systems are not built in a way that modularization or specialization are easy to identify. The general rule is to build a big software component that does everything and the modularization is poor, so we need to start from the very basics.

Let's start by writing some code, as shown in the following:

```
module.exports = function(options) {

  var init = {}

  /**
   * Sends one SMS
   */
  init.sendSMS = function(destination, content) {
    // Code to send SMS
  }

  /**
   * Reads the pending list of SMS.
   */
  init.readPendingSMS = function() {
    // code to receive SMS
    return listOfSms;
  }

  /**
   * Sends an email.
   */
  init.sendEmail = function(subject, content) {
    // code to send emails
  }

  /**
   * Gets a list of pending emails.
   */
  init.readPendingEmails = function() {
```

```
        // code to read the pending emails
        return listOfEmails;
    }


    /**
     * This code marks an email as read so it does not get
     * fetch again by the readPendingEmails function.
     */
    init.markEmailAsRead = function(messageId) {
        // code to mark a message as read.
    }


    /**
     * This function queues a document to be printed and
     * sent by post.
     */
    init.queuePost = function(document) {
        // code to queue post
    }


    return init;
}
```

As you can see, this module can be easily called **communications service** and it will be fairly easy to guess what it is doing. It manages the e-mail, SMS, and post communications.

This is probably too much. This service is deemed to grow out of control, as people will keep adding methods related to communications. This is the key problem of monolithic software: the bounded context spans across different areas, affecting the quality of our software from both functional and maintenance point of view.

If you are a software developer, a red flag will be raised straightaway: the cohesion of this module is quite poor.

Although it could have worked for a while, we are now changing our mindset. We are building small, scalable, and autonomous components that can be isolated. The cohesion in this case is bad as the module is doing too many different things: e-mail, SMS, and post.

What happens if we add another communication channel such as Twitter and Facebook notifications?

The service grows out of control. Instead of having small functional software components, you end up with a gigantic module that will be difficult to refactor, test, and modify. Let's take a look at the following SOLID design principles, explained in *Chapter 2, Microservices in Node.js – Seneca and PM2 Alternatives*:

- **Single-responsibility principle**: The module does too many things.

- **Open for extension, closed for modification**: The module will need to be modified to add new functionalities and probably change the common code.

- **Liskov Substitution**: We will skip this one again.

- **Interface segregation**: We don't have any interface specified in the module, just the implementation of an arbitrary set of functions.

- **Dependency injection:** There is no dependency injection. The module needs to be built by the calling code.

Things get more complicated if we don't have tests.

Therefore, let's split it into various small modules using Seneca.

First, the e-mail module (`email.js`) will be as follows:

```
module.exports = function (options) {

  /**
   * Sends an email.
   */
  this.add({channel: 'email', action: 'send'}, function(msg,
    respond) {
    // Code to send an email.
    respond(null, {...});
  });

  /**
   * Gets a list of pending emails.
   */
  this.add({channel: 'email', action: 'pending'}, function(msg,
    respond) {
    // Code to read pending email.
    respond(null, {...});
  });

  /**
   * Marks a message as read.
   */
```

```
      this.add({channel: 'email', action: 'read'}, function(msg,
        respond) {
        // Code to mark a message as read.
        respond(null, {...});
      });
    }
```

The SMS module (sms.js) will be as follows:

```
module.exports = function (options) {

  /**
   * Sends an email.
   */
  this.add({channel: 'sms', action: 'send'}, function(msg,
    respond) {
    // Code to send a sms.
    respond(null, {...});
  });

  /**
   * Receives the pending SMS.
   */
  this.add({channel: 'sms', action: 'pending'}, function(msg,
    respond) {
    // Code to read pending sms.
    respond(null, {...});
  });
}
```

Finally, the post module (post.js) will be as follows:

```
module.exports = function (options) {

  /**
   * Queues a post message for printing and sending.
   */
  this.add({channel: 'post', action: 'queue'}, function(msg,
    respond) {
    // Code to queue a post message.
    respond(null, {...});
  });
}
```

The following diagram shows the new structure of modules:

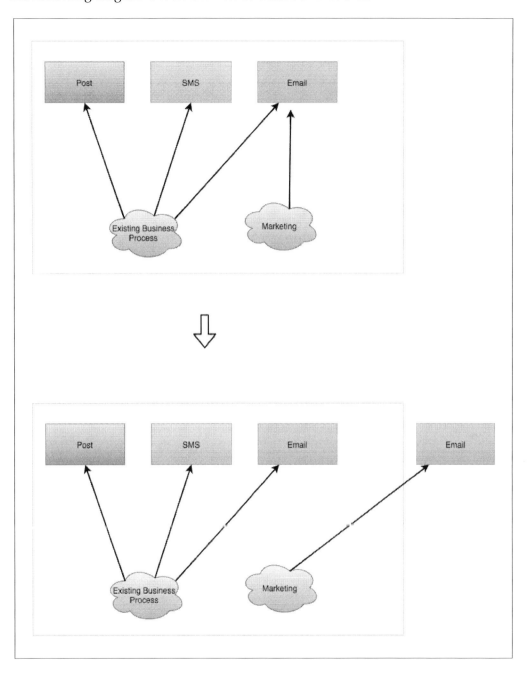

Now, we have three modules. Each one of these modules does one specific thing without interfering with each other; we have created high-cohesion modules.

Let's run the preceding code, as follows:

```
var seneca = require("seneca")()
        .use("email")
        .use("sms")
        .use("post");


seneca.listen({port: 1932, host: "10.0.0.7"});
```

As simple as that, we have created a server with the IP 10.0.0.7 bound that listens on the 1932 port for incoming requests. As you can see, we haven't referenced any file, we just referenced the module by name; Seneca will do the rest.

Let's run it and verify that Seneca has loaded the plugins:

node index.js --seneca.log.all | grep DEFINE

This command will output something similar to the following lines:

```
2015-11-12T22:57:24.720Z bml3vuxw8qjv/1447369044687/7355/- DEBUG plugin basic      DEFINE {}
2015-11-12T22:57:24.790Z bml3vuxw8qjv/1447369044687/7355/- DEBUG plugin transport DEFINE {}
2015-11-12T22:57:24.832Z bml3vuxw8qjv/1447369044687/7355/- DEBUG plugin web        DEFINE {}
2015-11-12T22:57:24.847Z bml3vuxw8qjv/1447369044687/7355/- DEBUG plugin mem-store DEFINE {}
2015-11-12T22:57:24.860Z bml3vuxw8qjv/1447369044687/7355/- DEBUG plugin email      DEFINE {}
2015-11-12T22:57:24.872Z bml3vuxw8qjv/1447369044687/7355/- DEBUG plugin sms        DEFINE {}
2015-11-12T22:57:24.882Z bml3vuxw8qjv/1447369044687/7355/- DEBUG plugin post       DEFINE {}
```

If you remember from *Chapter 2, Microservices in Node.js – Seneca and PM2 Alternatives*, Seneca loads a few plugins by default: basic, transport, web, and mem-store, which allow Seneca to work out of the box without being hassled with the configuration. Obviously, as we will see in *Chapter 4, Writing Your First Microservice in Node.js*, that the configuration is necessary as, for example, mem-store will only store data in the memory without persisting it between executions.

Aside from the standard plugins, we can see that Seneca has loaded three extra plugins: email, sms, and post, which are the plugins that we have created.

As you can see, the services written in Seneca are quite easy to understand once you know how the framework works. In this case, I have written the code in the form of a plugin so that it can be used by different instances of Seneca on different machines, as Seneca has a transparent transport mechanism that allows us to quickly redeploy and scale parts of our monolithic app as microservices, as follows:

- The new version can be easily tested, as changes on the e-mail functionality will only affect sending the e-mail.

- It is easy to scale. As we will see in the next chapter, replicating a service is as easy as configuring a new server and pointing our Seneca client to it.

- It is also easy to maintain, as the software is easier to understand and modify.

Disadvantages

With microservices, we solve the biggest problems in modern enterprise, but that does not mean that they are problem free. Microservices often lead to different types of problems that are not easy to foresee.

The first and most concerning one is the operational overhead that could chew up the benefits obtained from using microservices. When you are designing a system, you should always have one question in mind: how to automate this? Automation is the key to tackling this problem.

The second disadvantage with microservices is nonuniformity on the applications. A team might consider something a good practice that could be banned in another team (especially around exception handling), which adds an extra layer of isolation between teams that probably does not do well for the communication of your engineers within the team.

Lastly, but not less important, microservices introduce a bigger communication complexity that could lead to security problems. Instead of having to control a single application and its communication with the outer world, we are now facing a number of servers that communicate with each other.

Splitting the monolith

Consider that the marketing department of your company has decided to run an aggressive e-mail campaign that is going to require peaks of capacity that could harm the normal day-to-day process of sending e-mail. Under stress, the e-mails will be delayed and that could cause us problems.

Luckily, we have built our system as explained in the previous section. Small Seneca modules in the form of a high-cohesion and low-coupled plugins.

Then, the solution to achieve it is simple: deploy the e-mail service (`email.js`) on more than one machine:

```
var seneca = require("seneca")().use("email");
seneca.listen({port: 1932, host: "new-email-service-ip"});
```

Also, create a Seneca client pointing to it, as follows:

```
var seneca = require("seneca")()
      .use("email")
      .use("sms")
      .use("post");
seneca.listen({port: 1932, host: "10.0.0.7"});

// interact with the existing email service using "seneca"

var senecaEmail = require("seneca").client({host: "new-email-
   service-ip", port: 1932});

// interact with the new email service using "senecaEmail"
```

From now on, the `senecaEmail` variable will contact the remote service when calling `act` and we would have achieved our goal: *scale up our first microservice.*

Problems splitting the monolith – it is all about the data

Data storage could be problematic. If your application has grown out of control for a number of years, the database would have done the same, and by now, the organic growth will make it hard to deal with significant changes in the database.

Microservices should look after their own data. Keeping the data local to the service is one of the keys to ensure that the system remains flexible as it evolves, but it might not be always possible. As an example, financial services suffer especially from one of the main weak points of microservices-oriented architectures: *the lack of transactionality.* When a software component deals with money, it needs to ensure that the data remains consistent and not eventually consistent after every single operation. If a customer deposits money in a financial company, the software that holds the account balance needs to be consistent with the money held in the bank, otherwise, the reconciliation of the accounts will fail. Not only that, if your company is a regulated entity, it could cause serious problems for the continuity of the business.

The general rule of thumb, when working with microservices and financial systems, is to keep a not-so-microservice that deals with all the money and creates microservices for the auxiliary modules of the system such as e-mailing, SMS, user registration, and so on, as shown in the following image:

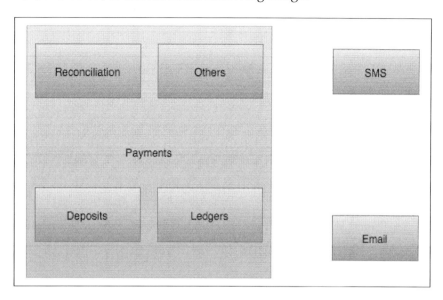

As you can see in the preceding picture, the fact that payments will be a big microservice instead of smaller services, it only has implications in the operational side, there is nothing preventing us from modularizing the application as seen before. The fact that withdrawing money from an ATM has to be an atomic operation (either succeed or fail without intermediate status) should not dictate how we organize the code in our application, allowing us to modularize the services, but spanning the transaction scope across all of them.

Organizational alignment

In a company where the software is built based on microservices, every single stakeholder needs to be involved in decision making.

Microservices are a huge paradigm shift. Usually, large organizations tend to build software in a very old fashioned manner. Big releases every few months that require days to complete the **quality assurance** (**QA**) phase and few hours to deploy.

When a company chooses to implement a microservices-oriented architecture, the methodology changes completely: small teams work on small features that are built, tested, and deployed on their own. The teams do one thing (one microservice, or more realistic, a few of them) and they do it well (they master the domain and technical knowledge required to build the software).

These are what usually called cross-functional teams. A unit of work of few people that have the required knowledge to build high-quality software components.

It is also important to flag that the team has to master the domain knowledge needed to understand the business requirements.

Here is where the majority of the companies where I have worked in my professional life fail (in my opinion). Developers are considered brick stackers that magically understand the business flows without being exposed to them before. If one developer delivers X amount of work in one week, ten developers will deliver $10X$. This is wrong.

People in cross-functional teams that build the microservices have to master (not only know) the domain-specific knowledge in order to be efficient and factor the Conway's Law and its implications into the system for changing how the business processes work.

When talking about organizational alignment in microservices, autonomy is the key. The teams need to be autonomous in order to be agile while building the microservices, which implies keeping the technical authority within the team, as follows:

- Languages used
- Code standards
- Patterns used to solve problems
- Tools chosen to build, test, debug, and deploy the software

This is an important part, as this is where we need to define how the company builds software and where the engineering problems may be introduced.

As an example, we can look into the coding standards, as shown in the following list:

- Do we want to keep the same coding standards across the teams?
- Do we want each team to have their own coding standards?

In general, I am always in favor of the 80% rule: *80% of perfection is more than enough for 100% of the use cases*. It means that loosening up the coding standards (it can be applied to other areas) and allowing some level of imperfection/personalization, helps to reduce the friction between teams and also allows the engineers to quickly catch up with the very few important rules to follow such as logging strategies or exception handling.

If your coding standards are too complicated, there will be friction when a team tries to push a code into a microservice out of their usual scope (remember, teams own the services, but every team can contribute to them).

Summary

In this chapter, we discussed the principles of building monolithic applications oriented to be split as microservices, depending on the business needs. As you have learned, the **Atomicity**, **Consistency**, **Isolation**, **Durability** (**ACID**) design principles are concepts that we need to have in mind in order to build high quality software.

You have also learned that we cannot assume that we are going to be able to design a system from scratch, so we need to be smart about how we build the new parts of the system and how we refactor the existing ones so that we achieve the level of flexibility required to satisfy the business needs and be resilient.

We also have given a small introduction about monolithic designed databases and how they are the biggest pain points when splitting a monolithic software into microservices, as it is usually required to shut down the system for a few hours in order to split the data into local databases. This subject could well be an entire book as new trends with NoSQL databases are changing the game of data storage.

Finally, we discussed how to align the teams of engineers in our company in order to be efficient while keeping the flexibility and resilience needed to be able to be agile, as well as how the Conway's Law impacts the conversion of monolithic systems into microservices-oriented architectures.

In the next chapter, we will apply all the principles discussed in the first three chapters, as well as a big dose of common sense to build a full working system based on microservices.

4

Writing Your First Microservice in Node.js

We have been learning about how to build robust microservices-oriented software, and now it is time to put all the concepts to practice. In this chapter, we are going to build a microservices-oriented e-commerce using Seneca and some other frameworks that are going to allow us to write a software that will benefit from the particularities of the microservices.

Micromerce – the big picture

It covers the following:

- Writing microservices

- Sizing microservices

- Creating APIs

- Integrating Seneca with Express

- Storing data using Seneca

In this chapter, we are going to write a full (nearly) simplistic e-commerce solution based on microservices. Full means full from the conceptual point of view, but for obvious reasons, it won't be full (as production ready) as it could take us a few books to handle all the possible flows.

We won't go deep in to the UI, as it is not related to the subject of this book. What we will do instead is a microservice that will aggregate all the other microservices, creating a frontend API to be consumed by a **Single-Page Application** (**SPA**), built with any of the modern JavaScript frameworks.

In this chapter, we are going to develop the following four microservices:

- **Product Manager**: This microservice will be responsible for adding, editing, and removing products from our database, as well as serving products to the customers. This microservice will be partially public for a potential admin site to add/remove products.

- **Order Manager**: This microservice will be responsible for managing the order and billing.

- **Emailer**: This microservice will be responsible for delivering e-mails to the customers.

- **UI**: This microservice will expose the feature from the other microservices to a potential SPA, but we will only build the JSON interface.

Building the four preceding microservices, we will develop the concepts discussed in the previous chapters so that, by the end of this chapter, we will be able to identify the most common pitfalls going forward. Keep in mind that the objective of this book is not converting you into a microservices or Node.js expert, but to give you the tools required to learn by yourself, as well as make you aware of the best design principles and the most common pitfalls.

Let's take a look at the deployment diagram:

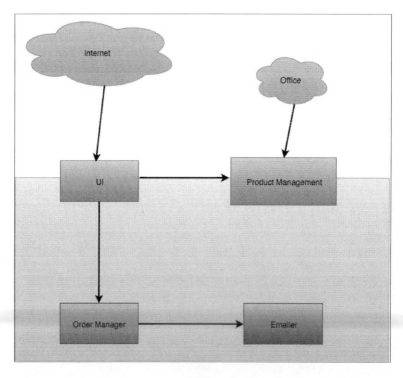

This diagram shows how our company (the yellow square) hides some of our microservices from the real world and exposes some others to different networks, as follows:

- **UI** will be exposed to the Internet. Everybody will be able to hit this endpoint.

- **Product Management** will manage the products in our e-commerce. It will have the following two interfaces:
    - A Seneca endpoint from where the UI will extract data
    - A JSON API from where the office of our company will be able to create, update, and delete products

- **Emailer** will be our communication channel with our customers. We will use this microservice to explain the good points of Seneca, and we will also give an example of the eventual consistency and system degradation when a microservice fails.

- **Order Manager**: This microservice will let us handle the orders for our customers. With this microservice, we will discuss how to handle the fact that the data is local to each microservice, instead of being global to the system. You can't just go to the database to recover the product name or price, it needs to be recovered from other microservice.

 As you can see, there is no user or staff management, but with these four microservices, we will be able to develop the core concepts of microservices architectures. Seneca comes with a very powerful data and transport plugin system that makes it easy to use Seneca with different data storages and transport systems.

For all our microservices, we are going to use MongoDB as the storage. Seneca comes with an out-of-the-box in-memory database plugin that allows you to start coding straightaway, but the storage is transient: it does not persist the data between calls.

Product Manager – the two-faced core

Product Manager is the core of our system. I know what you are thinking: microservices should be small (micro) and distributed (no central point), but you need to set the conceptual centre somewhere, otherwise you will end up with a fragmented system and traceability problems (we will talk about it later).

Building a dual API with Seneca is fairly easy, as it comes with a quite straightforward integration with Express. Express is going to be used to expose some capabilities of the UI such as editing products, adding products, deleting products, and so on. It is a very convenient framework, easy to learn, and it integrates well with Seneca. It is also a de-facto standard on Node.js for web apps, so it makes it easy to find information about the possible problems.

It is going to also have a private part exposed through Seneca TCP (the default plugin in Seneca) so that our internal network of microservices (specifically, the UI) will be able to access the list of products in our catalogue.

Product Manager is going to be small and cohesioned (it will only manage products), as well as scalable, but it will hold all the knowledge required to deal with products in our e-commerce.

First thing we need to do is to define our Product Manager microservice, as follows:

- This is going to have a function to retrieve all the products in the database. This is probably a bad idea in a production system (as it probably would require pagination), but it works for our example.

- This should have one function that fetches all the products for a given category. It is similar to the previous one, it would need pagination in a production-ready system.

- This should have a function to retrieve products by identifier (id).

- This should have one function that allows us to add products to the database (in this case MongoDB). This function will use the Seneca data abstraction to decouple our microservice from the storage: we will be able to (in theory) switch Mongo to a different database without too much hassle (in theory again).

- This should have one function to remove products. Again, using Seneca data abstraction.

- This should have one function to edit products.

Our product will be a data structure having four fields: **name**, **category**, **description**, and **price**. As you can see, it is a bit simplistic, but it will help us to understand the complicated world of microservices.

Our Product Management microservice is going to use MongoDB (https://www.mongodb.org/). Mongo is a document-oriented schema-less database that allows an enormous flexibility to store data such as products (that, at the end of the day, are documents). It is also a good choice for Node.js as it stores JSON objects, which is a standard, created for JavaScript (**JSON** stands for **JavaScript Object Notation**), so that looks like the perfect pairing.

There is a lot of useful information on the MongoDB website if you want to learn more about it.

Let's start coding our functions.

Fetching products

To fetch products, we go to the database and dump the full list of products straight to the interface. In this case, we won't create any pagination mechanism, but in general, paginating data is a good practice to avoid database (or applications, but mainly database) performance problems.

Let's see the following code:

```
/**
 * Fetch the list of all the products.
 */
seneca.add({area: "product", action: "fetch"}, function(args,
  done) {
  var products = this.make("products");
  products.list$({}, done);
});
```

We already have a pattern in Seneca that returns all the data in our database.

The `products.list$()` function will receive the following two parameters:

- The query criteria
- A function that receives an error and result object (remember the error-first callback approach)

Seneca uses the $ symbol to identify the key functions such as `list$`, `save$`, and so on. Regarding the naming of the properties of your objects, as long as you use alphanumeric identifiers, your naming will be collision free.

We are passing the `done` function from the `seneca.add()` method to the `list$` method. This works as Seneca follows the callback with error-first approach. In other words, we are creating a shortcut for the following code:

```
seneca.add({area: "product", action: "fetch"}, function(args,
  done) {
  var products = this.make("products");
  products.list$({}, function(err, result) {
    done(err, result);
  });
});
```

Fetching by category

Fetching by category is very similar to fetching the full list of products. The only difference is that now the Seneca action will take a parameter to filter the products by category.

Let's see the code:

```
/**
 * Fetch the list of products by category.
 */
seneca.add({area: "product", action: "fetch", criteria:
    "byCategory"}, function(args, done) {
    var products = this.make("products");
    products.list$({category: args.category}, done);
});
```

One of the first questions that most advanced developers will now have in their mind is that *isn't this a perfect scenario for an injection attack?* Well, Seneca is smart enough to prevent it, so we don't need to worry about it any more than avoid concatenating strings with user input.

As you can see, the only significant difference is the parameter passed called `category`, which gets delegated into Seneca data abstraction layer that will generate the appropriate query, depending on the storage we use. This is extremely powerful when talking about microservices. If you remember, in the previous chapters, we always talked about coupling as if it was the root of all evils, and now we can assure it is, and Seneca handles it in a very elegant way. In this case, the framework provides a contract that the different storage plugins have to satisfy in order to work. In the preceding example, `list$` is part of this contract. If you use the Seneca storage wisely, switching your microservice over to a new database engine (have you ever been tempted to move a part of your data over MongoDB?) is a matter of configuration.

Fetching by ID

Fetching a product by ID is one of the most necessary methods, and it is also a tricky one. Not tricky from the coding point of view, as shown in the following:

```
/**
 * Fetch a product by id.
 */
seneca.add({area: "product", action: "fetch", criteria: "byId"},
    function(args, done) {
    var product = this.make("products");
    product.load$(args.id, done);
});
```

The tricky part is how `id` is generated. The generation of `id` is one of the contact points with the database. Mongo creates a hash to represent a synthetic ID; whereas, MySQL usually creates an integer that auto-increments to uniquely identify each record. Given that, if we want to switch MongoDB to MySQL in one of our apps, the first problem that we need to solve is how to map a hash that looks something similar to the following into an ordinal number:

```
e777d434a849760a1303b7f9f989e33a
```

In 99% of the cases, this is fine, but we need to be careful, especially when storing IDs as, if you recall from the previous chapters, the data should be local to each microservice, which could imply that changing the data type of the ID of one entity, requires changing the referenced ID in all the other databases.

Adding a product

Adding a product is trivial. We just need to create the data and save it in the database:

```
/**
 * Adds a product.
 */
seneca.add({area: "product", action: "add"}, function(args, done) {
  var products = this.make("products");
  products.category = args.category;
  products.name = args.name;
  products.description = args.description;
  products.category = args.category;
  products.price = args.price;
  products.save$(function(err, product) {
    done(err, products.data$(false));
  });
});
```

In this method, we are using a helper from Seneca, `products.data$(false)`. This helper will allow us to retrieve the data of the entity without all the metadata about namespace (zone), entity name, and base name that we are not interested in when the data is returned to the calling method.

Removing a product

The removal of a product is usually done by `id`: We target the specific data that we want to remove by the primary key and then remove it, as follows:

```
/**
 * Removes a product by id.
 */
seneca.add({area: "product", action: "remove"}, function(args,
  done) {
  var product = this.make("products");
  product.remove$(args.id, function(err) {
  done(err, null);
  });
});
```

In this case, we don't return anything aside from an error if something goes wrong, so the endpoint that calls this action can assume that a non-errored response is a success.

Editing a product

We need to provide an action to edit products. The code for doing that is as follows:

```
/**
 * Edits a product fetching it by id first.
 */
seneca.edit({area: "product", action: "edit"}, function(args,
  done) {
  seneca.act({area: "product", action: "fetch", criteria: "byId",
  id: args.id}, function(err, result) {
  result.data$(
  {
    name: args.name,
    category: args.category,
    description: args.description,
    price: args.price
  }
  );
  result.save$(function(err, product){
    done(product.data$(false));
    });
  });
});
```

Here is an interesting scenario. Before editing a product, we need to fetch it by ID, and we have already done that. So, what we are doing here is relying on the already existing action to retrieve a product by ID, copying the data across, and saving it.

This is a nice way for code reuse introduced by Seneca, where you can delegate a call from one action to another and work in the wrapper action with the result.

Wiring everything up

As we agreed earlier, the product manager is going to have two faces: one that will be exposed to other microservices using the Seneca transport over TCP and a second one exposed through Express (a Node.js library to create web apps) in the REST way.

Let's wire everything together:

```
var plugin = function(options) {
  var seneca = this;

  /**
   * Fetch the list of all the products.
   */
  seneca.add({area: "product", action: "fetch"}, function(args,
    done) {
    var products = this.make("products");
    products.list$({}, done);
  });

  /**
   * Fetch the list of products by category.
   */
  seneca.add({area: "product", action: "fetch", criteria:
    "byCategory"}, function(args, done) {
    var products = this.make("products");
    products.list$({category: args.category}, done);
  });

  /**
   * Fetch a product by id.
   */
  seneca.add({area: "product", action: "fetch", criteria: "byId"},
    function(args, done) {
    var product = this.make("products");
```

```
    product.load$(args.id, done);
});

/**
 * Adds a product.
 */
seneca.add({area: "product", action: "add"}, function(args,
  done) {
  var products = this.make("products");
  products.category = args.category;
  products.name = args.name;
  products.description = args.description;
  products.category = args.category;
  products.price = args.price;
  products.save$(function(err, product) {
    done(err, products.data$(false));
  });
});

/**
 * Removes a product by id.
 */
seneca.add({area: "product", action: "remove"}, function(args,
  done) {
  var product = this.make("products");
  product.remove$(args.id, function(err) {
    done(err, null);
  });
});

/**
 * Edits a product fetching it by id first.
 */
seneca.add({area: "product", action: "edit"}, function(args,
  done) {
  seneca.act({area: "product", action: "fetch", criteria:
    "byId", id: args.id}, function(err, result) {
    result.data$(
      {
        name: args.name,
        category: args.category,
        description: args.description,
        price: args.price
      }
    );
```

```
      result.save$(function(err, product){
        done(err, product.data$(false));
      });
    });
  });
}
module.exports = plugin;

var seneca = require("seneca")();
seneca.use(plugin);
seneca.use("mongo-store", {
  name: "seneca",
  host: "127.0.0.1",
  port: "27017"
});

seneca.ready(function(err){

  seneca.act('role:web',{use:{
    prefix: '/products',
    pin: {area:'product',action:'*'},
    map:{
    fetch: {GET:true},
    edit: {GET:false,POST:true},
    delete: {GET: false, DELETE: true}
    }
  }});
  var express = require('express');
  var app = express();
  app.use(require("body-parser").json());

  // This is how you integrate Seneca with Express
  app.use( seneca.export('web') );

  app.listen(3000);

});
```

Now let's explain the code:

We have created a Seneca plugin. This plugin can be reused across different microservices. This plugin contains all the definitions of methods needed by our microservice that we have previously described.

The preceding code describes the following two sections:

- The first few lines connect to Mongo. In this case, we are specifying that Mongo is a local database. We are doing that through the use of a plugin called mongo-store—https://github.com/rjrodger/seneca-mongo-store, written by Richard Rodger, the author of Seneca.

- The second part is new to us. It might sound familiar if you have used JQuery before, but basically what the seneca.ready() callback is doing is taking care of the fact that Seneca might not have connected to Mongo before the calls start flowing into its API. The seneca.ready() callback is where the code for integrating Express with Seneca lives.

The following is the package.json configuration of our app:

```
{
  "name": "Product Manager",
  "version": "1.0.0",
  "description": "Product Management sub-system",
  "main": "index.js",
  "keywords": [
    "microservices",
    "products"
  ],
  "author": "David Gonzalez",
  "license": "ISC",
  "dependencies": {
  "body-parser": "^1.14.1",
  "debug": "^2.2.0",
  "express": "^4.13.3",
  "seneca": "^0.8.0",
  "seneca-mongo-store": "^0.2.0",
  "type-is": "^1.6.10"
  }
}
```

Here we control all the libraries needed for our microservice to run, as well as the configuration.

Integrating with Express – how to create a REST API

Integrating with Express is quite straightforward. Let's take a look at the code:

```
seneca.act('role:web',{use:{
  prefix: '/products',
  pin: {area:'product',action:'*'},
  map:{
  fetch: {GET:true},
  edit: {PUT:true},
  delete: {GET: false, DELETE: true}
  }
}});
var express = require('express');
var app = express();
app.use(require("body-parser").json());

// This is how you integrate Seneca with Express
app.use( seneca.export('web') );

app.listen(3000);
```

This code snippet, as we've seen in the preceding section, provides the following three REST endpoints:

/products/fetch

/products/edit

/products/delete

Let's explain how.

First, what we do is tell Seneca to execute the role:web action, indicating the configuration. This configuration specifies to use a /products prefix for all the URLs, and it pins the action with a matching {area: "product", action: "*"} pattern. This is also new for us, but it is a nice way to specify to Seneca that whatever action it executes in the URL, it will have implicit area: "product" of the handler. This means that /products/fetch endpoint will correspond to the {area: 'products', action: 'fetch'} pattern. This could be a bit difficult, but once you get used to it, it is actually really powerful. It does not force use to fully couple our actions with our URLs by conventions.

In the configuration, the attribute map specifies the HTTP actions that can be executed over an endpoint: fetch will allow GET, edit will allow PUT, and delete will only allow DELETE. This way, we can control the semantics of the application.

Everything else is probably familiar to you. Create an Express app and specify using the following two plugins:

- The JSON body parser
- The Seneca web plugin

This is all. Now, if we add a new action to our Seneca list of actions in order to expose it through the API, the only thing that needs to be done is to modify the map attribute to allow HTTP methods.

Although we have built a very simplistic microservice, it captures a big portion of the common patterns that you find when creating a **CRUD** (**Create Read Update Delete**) application. We have also created a small REST API out of a Seneca application with little to no effort. All we need to do now is configure the infrastructure (MongoDB) and we are ready to deploy our microservice.

The e-mailer – a common problem

E-mailing is something that every company needs to do. We need to communicate with our customers in order to send notifications, bills, or registration e-mails.

In the companies where I've worked before, e-mailing always presented a problem such as e-mails not being delivered, or being delivered twice, with the wrong content to the wrong customer, and so on. It looks terrifying that something as simple as sending an e-mail could be this complicated to manage.

In general, e-mail communication is the first candidate to write a microservice. Think about it:

- E-mail does one thing
- E-mail does it well
- E-mail keeps its own data

It is also a good example of how the *Conway's law* kicks into our systems without being noticed. We design our systems modeling the existing communication in our company as we are constrained by it.

How to send e-mails

Back to the basics. How do we send e-mails? I am not talking about which network protocol we use for sending the e-mail or what are the minimum acceptable headers?

I am talking about what we need to send an e-mail from the business point of view:

- A title
- The content
- A destination address

That is everything. We could have gone far, talking about acknowledgements, secure e-mail, BCCs, and so on. However, we are following the lean methodology: start with the minimum viable product and build up from it until you achieve the desired result.

I can't remember a project where the e-mail sending wasn't a controversial part. The product chosen to deliver e-mails ends up tightly coupled to the system and it is really hard to replace it seamlessly. However, microservices are here to rescue us.

Defining the interface

As I mentioned before, although it sounds easy, sending corporate e-mails could end up being a mess. Therefore, the first thing we need to clear is our minimum requirements:

- How do we render the e-mail?
    - Does rendering the email belongs to the bound context of the email manipulation?
    - Do we create another microservice to render e-mails?
    - Do we use a third party to manage the e-mails?
- Do we store the already sent e-mails for auditing purposes?

For this microservice, we are going to use Mandrill. Mandrill is a company that allows us to send corporate e-mails, track the already sent e-mails, and create e-mail templates that can be edited online.

Our microservice is going to look as shown in the following code:

```
var plugin = function(options) {
  var seneca = this;
  /**
```

```
    * Sends an email using a template email.
    */
  seneca.add({area: "email", action: "send", template: "*"},
     function(args, done) {
// TODO: More code to come.
  });

  /**
    * Sends an email including the content.
    */
  seneca.add({area: "email", action: "send"}, function(args, done) {
// TODO: More code to come.
  });
};
```

We have two patterns: one that makes use of templates and the other that sends the content contained in the request.

As you can see, everything that we have defined here is information related to e-mailing. There is no bleeding from the Mandrill terminology into what the other microservices see in our e-mail sending. The only compromise that we are making is the templating. We are delegating the template rendering to the e-mail sender, but it is not a big deal, as even if we walk away from Mandrill, we will need to render the content somehow.

We will come back to the code later.

Setting up Mandrill

Mandrill is fairly easy to use and shouldn't be a problem to set up. However, we are going to use the test mode so that we can assure that the e-mails are not going to be delivered and we can access the API for all our needs.

The first thing we need to do is create an account on Mandrill. Just register with your e-mail at https://mandrillapp.com, and you should be able to access to it, as shown in the following screenshot:

Now we have created an account that we need to enter into the test mode. In order to do it, just click on your e-mail at the top-right corner and select the **Turn on the test mode** option from the menu. The Mandrill menu on the left will turn orange now.

Next, we need to create an API key. This key is the login information to be used by the Mandrill API. Just click on **Settings** and **SMTP & API Info** and add a new key (don't forget the checkbox to mark the key as test key). It should look like the following screenshot now:

The key is everything you need for now. Let's test the API:

```
var mandrill = require("mandrill-api/mandrill");
var mandrillClient = new mandrill.Mandrill("<YOUR-KEY-HERE>");

mandrillClient.users.info({}, function(result){
  console.log(result);
}, function(e){
  console.log(e);
});
```

With these few lines, we have managed to test that Mandrill is up and running and we have a valid key. The output of this program should be something very similar to the following JSON:

```
{ username: 'youremail@yourdomain.com',
  created_at: '2015-12-05 10:55:59.02874',
  public_id: 'yourpublicid',
  reputation: 33,
  hourly_quota: 25,
  backlog: 0,
  stats:
   { today:
      { sent: 0,
        hard_bounces: 0,
        soft_bounces: 0,
        rejects: 0,
        complaints: 0,
<...continues...>
```

Hands on – integrating Mandrill in your microservice

Everything is ready now. We have a working key and our interface. The only thing left is to create the code. We are going to use a small part of the Mandrill API, but if you want to make use of other features, you can find a better description here: https://mandrillapp.com/api/docs/

Let's take a look at the following code:

```
/**
 * Sends an email including the content.
 */
```

```
seneca.add({area: "email", action: "send"}, function(args, done)
  {
  console.log(args);
  var message = {
    "html": args.content,
    "subject": args.subject,
    "to": [{
      "email": args.to,
      "name": args.toName,
      "type": "to"
    }],
    "from_email": "info@micromerce.com",
    "from_name": "Micromerce"
  }
  mandrillClient.messages.send({"message": message},
    function(result) {
    done(null, {status: result.status});
  }, function(e) {
    done({code: e.name}, null);
  });
});
```

This first method sends messages without using a template. We just get the HTML content (and a few other parameters) from our application and deliver it through Mandrill.

As you can see, we only have two contact points with the outer world: the parameters passed in and the return of our actions. Both of them have a clear contract that has nothing to do with Mandrill, but what about the data?

At the error, we are returning e.name, assuming that it is a code. At some point, someone will end up branching the flow depending on this **error code**. Here, we have something called data coupling; our software components don't depend on the contract, but they do depend on the content sent across.

Now, the question is: how do we fix it? *We can't*. At least not in an easy way. We need to assume that our microservice is not perfect, it has a flaw. If we switch provider for e-mailing, we are going to need to revisit the calling code to check potential couplings.

In the world of software, in every single project that I've worked on before, there was always a big push trying to make the code as generic as possible, trying to guess the future, which usually could be as bad as assuming that your microservice won't be perfect. There is something that always attracted my attention: we put a large amount of effort in to perfection, but we pretty much ignore the fact that we are going to fail and we do can nothing about it. Software fails often and we need to be prepared for that.

Later, we will see a pattern to factor human nature into the microservices: **the circuit breaker**.

Don't be surprised if Mandrill rejects the e-mails due to the *unsigned* reason. This is due to the fact that they couldn't validate the domain from where we are sending the e-mail (in this case, a dummy domain that does not exist). If we want Mandrill to actually process the e-mails (even though we are in test mode), we just need to verify our domain by adding some configuration to it.

 More information can be found in the Mandrill documentation here: `https://mandrillapp.com/api/docs/`

The second method to send e-mails is send an e-mail from a template. In this case, Mandrill provides a flexible API:

- It provides per-recipient variables in case we send the e-mail to a list of customers
- It has global variables
- It allows content replacement (we can replace a full section)

For convenience, we are going to just use global variables as we are limited on space in this book.

Let's take a look at the following code:

```
/**
 * Sends an email using a template email.
 */
seneca.add({area: "email", action: "send", template: "*"},
  function(args, done) {
  console.log("sending");
  var message = {
    "subject": args.subject,
    "to": [{
      "email": args.to,
```

```
        "name": args.toName,
        "type": "to"
      }],
      "from_email": "info@micromerce.com",
      "from_name": "Micromerce",
      "global_merge_vars": args.vars,
    }
    mandrillClient.messages.sendTemplate(
      {"template_name": args.template, "template_content": {},
        "message": message},
    function(result) {
      done(null, {status: result.status});
    }, function(e) {
      done({code: e.name}, null);
    });
  });
```

Now we can create our templates in Mandrill (and let someone else to manage them) and we are able to use them to send e-mails. Again, we are specializing. Our system specializes in sending e-mails and you leave the creation of the e-mails to someone else (maybe someone from the marketing team who knows how to talk to customers).

Let's analyze this microservice:

- **Data is stored locally**: Not really (it is stored in Mandrill), but from the design point of view, it is

- **Our microservice is well cohesioned**: It sends only e-mails; it does one thing, and does it well

- **The size of the microservice is correct**: It can be understood in a few minutes, it does not have unnecessary abstractions and can be rewritten fairly easily

When we talked about the SOLID design principles earlier, we always skipped L, which stands for **Liskov Substitution**. Basically, this means that the software has to be semantically correct. For example, if we write an object-oriented program that handles one abstract class, the program has to be able to handle all the subclasses.

Coming back to Node.js, if our service is able to handle sending a plain e-mail, it should be easy to extend and add capabilities without modifying the existing ones.

Think about it from the day-to-day production operations point of view; if a new feature is added to your system, the last thing you want to do is retest the existing functionalities or even worse, deliver the feature to production, introducing a bug that no one was aware of.

Let's create a use case. We want to send the same e-mail to two recipients. Although Mandrill API allows the calling code to do it, we haven't factored in a potential CC.

Therefore, we are going to add a new action in Seneca that allows us to do it, as follows:

```
/**
 * Sends an email including the content.
 */
seneca.add({area: "email", action: "send", cc: "*"},
  function(args, done) {
  var message = {
    "html": args.content,
    "subject": args.subject,
    "to": [{
      "email": args.to,
      "name": args.toName,
      "type": "to"
    },{
      "email": args.cc,
      "name": args.ccName,
      "type": "cc"
    }],
    "from_email": "info@micromerce.com",
    "from_name": "Micromerce"
  }
  mandrillClient.messages.send({"message": message},
    function(result) {
    done(null, {status: result.status});
  }, function(e) {
    done({code: e.name}, null);
  });
});
```

We have instructed Seneca to take the calls that include cc in the list of parameters and send them using a Mandrill CC in the send API. If we want to use it, the following signature of the calling code will change:

```
seneca.act({area: "email", action: "send", subject: "The Subject", to:
"test@test.com", toName: "Test Testingtong"}, function(err, result){
// More code here
});
```

The signature will change to the following code:

```
seneca.act({area: "email", action: "send", subject: "The Subject",
to: "test@test.com", toName: "Test Testingtong", cc: "test2@test.com",
ccName: "Test 2"}, function(err, result){
// More code here
});
```

If you remember correctly, the pattern matching tries to match the most concrete input so that if an action matches with more parameters than another one, the call will be directed to it.

Here is where Seneca shines: We can call it **polymorphism of actions**, as we can define different versions of the same action with different parameters that end up doing slightly different things and enabling us to reutilize the code if we are 100% sure that this is the right thing to do (remember, microservices enforce the share-nothing approach: repeating the code might not be as bad as coupling two actions).

Here is the `package.json` for the e-mailer microservice:

```
{
  "name": "emailing",
  "version": "1.0.0",
  "description": "Emailing sub-system",
  "main": "index.js",
  "keywords": [
  "microservices",
  "emailing"
  ],
  "author": "David Gonzalez",
  "license": "ISC",
  "dependencies": {
  "mandrill-api": "^1.0.45",
  "seneca": "^0.8.0"
  }
}
```

The fallback strategy

When you design a system, usually we think about replaceability of the existing components; for example, when using a persistence technology in Java, we tend to lean towards standards (**JPA**) so that we can replace the underlying implementation without too much effort.

Microservices take the same approach, but they isolate the problem instead of working towards an easy replaceability. If you read the preceding code, inside the Seneca actions, we have done nothing to hide the fact that we are using Mandrill to send the e-mails.

As I mentioned before, e-mailing is something that, although seems simple, always ends up giving problems.

Imagine that we want to replace Mandrill for a plain SMTP server such as Gmail. We don't need to do anything special, we just change the implementation and roll out the new version of our microservice.

The process is as simple as applying the following code:

```
var nodemailer = require('nodemailer');
var seneca = require("seneca")();
var transporter = nodemailer.createTransport({
  service: 'Gmail',
  auth: {
    user: 'info@micromerce.com',
    pass: 'verysecurepassword'
  }
});

/**
 * Sends an email including the content.
 */
seneca.add({area: "email", action: "send"}, function(args, done) {
  var mailOptions = {
    from: 'Micromerce Info <info@micromerce.com>',
    to: args.to,
    subject: args.subject,
    html: args.body
  };
  transporter.sendMail(mailOptions, function(error, info){
    if(error){
      done({code: e}, null);
    }
    done(null, {status: "sent"});
  });
});
```

For the outer world, our simplest version of the e-mail sender is now using SMTP through Gmail to deliver our e-mails.

As we will see later in the book, delivering a new version of the same interface in a microservice network is fairly easy; as long as we respect the interface, the implementation should be irrelevant.

We could even roll out one server with this new version and send some traffic to it in order to validate our implementation without affecting all the customers (in other words, contain the failure).

We have seen how to write an e-mail sender in this section. We have worked through a few examples on how our microservice can be adapted quickly for new requirements as soon as the business requires new capabilities or we decide that our vendor is not good enough to cope with our technical requirements.

The order manager

The order manager is a microservice that processes the orders that the customer places through the UI. As you probably remember, we are not going to create a sophisticated single-page application with a modern visual framework, as it is out of the scope of this book, but we are going to provide the JSON interface in order to be able to build the front end later.

Order manager introduces an interesting problem: this microservice needs access to the information about products, such as name, price, availability, and so on. However, it is stored in the product manager microservice, so how do we do that?

Well, the answer for this question might look simple, but requires a bit of thinking.

Defining the microservice – how to gather non-local data

Our microservice will need to do the following three things:

- Recover orders
- Create orders
- Delete existing orders

When recovering an order, the option is going to be simple. Recover the order by the primary key. We could extend it to recover orders by different criteria, such as price, date, and so on, but we are going to keep it simple as we want to focus on microservices.

When deleting existing orders, the option is also clear: use the ID to delete orders. Again, we could choose a more advanced deletion criteria, but we want to keep it simple.

The problem arises when we are trying to create orders. Creating an order in our small microservice architecture means sending an e-mail to the customer, specifying that we are processing their order, along with the details of the order, as follows:

- Number of products
- Price per product
- Total price
- Order ID (in case the customer needs to troubleshoot problems with the order)

How do we recover the product details?

If you see our diagram shown in the *Micromerce – the big picture* section of this chapter, order manager will only be called from the UI, which will be responsible to recover the product name, its price, and so on. We could adopt the following two strategies here:

- Order manager calls product manager and gets the details
- UI calls product manager and delegates the data to the order manager

Both options are totally valid, but in this case, we are going for the second: UI will gather the information needed to generate an order and it will only call the order manager when all the data required is available.

Now to answer the question: why?

A simple reason: failure tolerance. Let's take a look at the following sequence diagram of the two options:

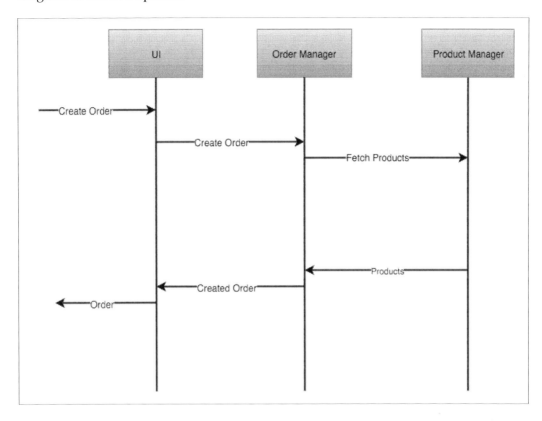

The diagram for the second option is shown as follows:

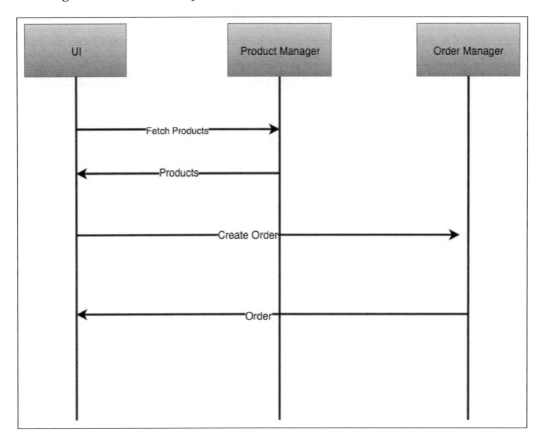

In the first view, there is a big difference: the depth of the call; whereas in the first example, we have two levels of depth (UI calls the order manager, which calls the product manager). In the second example, we have only one level of depth. There are a few immediate effects in our architecture, as follows:

- When something goes wrong, if we only have one level of depth, we don't need to check in too many places.

- We are more resilient. If something goes wrong, it is the UI of the microservice that notices it, returning the appropriate HTTP code, in this case, without having to translate the errors that occurred a few levels above the client-facing microservice.

- It is easier to deploy and test. Not much easier, but we don't need to juggle around, we can see straight away if the product manager is reached from the UI, instead of having to go through the order manager.

The fact that we are using this architecture instead of the two-level depth does not mean that it isn't appropriate for another situation: the network topology is something that you need to plan ahead if you are creating a microservices-oriented architecture, as it is one of the hardest aspects to change.

In some cases, if we want to be extremely flexible, we can use a messaging queue with publisher/subscriber technology where our microservices can subscribe to different types of messages and emit others to be consumed by a different service, but it could complicate the infrastructure that we need to put in place to avoid single point of failures.

The order manager – the code

Let's take a look at the code for the order manager:

```
var plugin = function(options) {
  var seneca = this;

  seneca.add({area: "orders", action: "fetch"}, function(args,
    done) {
    var orders = this.make("orders");
    orders.list$({id: args.id}, done);
  });

  seneca.add({area: "orders", action: "delete"}, function(args,
    done) {
    var orders = this.make("orders");
    orders.remove$({id: args.id}, function(err) {
        done(err, null);
    });
  });
}
module.exports = plugin;
```

As you can see, there is nothing complicated about the code. The only interesting point is the missing code from the create action.

Calling remote services

Until now, we have assumed that all our microservices run in the same machine, but that is far from ideal. In the real world, microservices are distributed and we need to use some sort of transport protocol to carry the message from one service to another.

Seneca, as well as nearForm, the company behind Seneca, has sorted this problem for us and the open source community around it.

As a modular system, Seneca has embedded the concept of plugin. By default, Seneca comes with a bundled plugin to use TCP as the protocol, but it is not hard to create a new transport plugin.

 While writing this book, I created one by myself: `https://github.com/dgonzalez/seneca-nservicebus-transport/`

With this plugin, we could route the Seneca messages through NServiceBus (a .NET-based Enterprise Bus), changing the configuration of our client and server.

Let's see how to configure Seneca to point to a different machine:

```
var senecaEmailer = require("seneca")().client({host: "192.168.0.2",
port: 8080});
```

By default, Seneca will use the default plugin for transport, which as we've seen in *Chapter 2, Microservices in Node.js – Seneca and PM2 Alternatives*, is `tcp`, and we have specified it to point to the `192.168.0.2` host on the `8080` port.

As simple as that, from now on, when we execute an act command on `senecaEmailer`, the transport will send the message across to the e-mailer and receives the response.

Let's see the rest of the code:

```
seneca.add({area: "orders", action: "create"}, function(args,
  done) {
  var products = args.products;
  var total = 0.0;
  products.forEach(function(product){
    total += product.price;
  });
  var orders = this.make("orders");
  orders.total = total;
  orders.customer_email = args.email;
  orders.customer_name = args.name;
  orders.save$(function(err, order) {
    var pattern = {
      area: "email",
      action: "send",
      template: "new_order",
      to: args.email,
      toName: args.name,
      vars: {
```

```
        // ... vars for rendering the template including the
            products ...
        }
      }
    senecaEmailer.act(pattern, done);
    });
  });
```

As you can see, we are receiving a list of products with all the data needed and passing them to the e-mailer to render the e-mail.

If we change the host where the e-mailer lives, the only change that we need to do here is the configuration of the `senecaEmailer` variable.

Even if we change the nature of the channel (we could potentially even write a plugin to send the data over Twitter, for example), the plugin should look after the particularities of it and be transparent for the application.

Resilience over perfection

In the example from the preceding section, we built a microservice that calls another microservice in order to resolve the call that it receives. However, the following points need to be kept in mind:

- What happens if the e-mailer is down?
- What happens if the configuration is wrong and the e-mailer is not working on the correct port?

We could be throwing *what ifs* for few pages.

Humans are imperfect and so are the things that they build, and software is not an exception. Humans are also bad at recognizing the potential problems in logical flows, and software tends to be a complex system.

In other languages, playing with exceptions is almost something normal, but in JavaScript, exceptions are a big deal:

- If an exception bubbles out in a web app in Java, it kills the current stack of calls and Tomcat (or the container that you use) returns an error to the client
- If an exception bubbles out in a Node.js app, the application is killed as we only have one thread executing the app

As you can see, pretty much every single callback in Node.js has a first parameter that is an error.

When talking about microservices, this error is especially important. You want to be resilient. The fact that an e-mail has failed sending does not mean that the order cannot be processed, but the e-mail could be manually sent later by someone reprocessing the data. This is what we call eventual consistency; we factor into our system the fact that at some point our system is going to crash.

In this case, if there is a problem sending the e-mail, but we could store the order in the database, the calling code, in this case the UI, should have enough information to decide whether the customer gets a fatal message or just a warning:

Your order is ready to be processed, however it might take us two days to send you the e-mail with the order details. Thanks for your patience.

Usually, the fact that our application will keep working even if we cannot complete a request, it is usually more business than technical decision. This is an important detail, as when building microservices, *Conway's law* is pushing us, the technical people, to model the existing business process and partial success maps perfectly to the human nature. If you can't complete a task, create a reminder in Evernote (or a similar tool) and come back to it once the blocker is resolved.

This reads much better than the following:

Something happened about something, but we can't tell you more (which is what my mind reads sometimes when I get a general failure in some websites).

We call this way of handling errors system degradation: it might not be 100% functional, but it will still work even though its few features are not available, instead of a general failure.

If you think for a second, how many times a web service call has rolled back a full transaction in your big corporate system only because it couldn't reach a third-party service that might not even be important?

In this section, we built a microservice that uses another microservice to resolve a request from a customer: order manager uses e-mailer to complete the request. We have also talked about resilience and how important it is in our architecture in order to provide the best service.

The UI – API aggregation

Until now, we have built independent microservices. They had a specific purpose and dealt with one specific part of our system: e-mail sending, product management, and order processing, but now we are building a microservice whose only purpose is to facilitate the communication between microservices.

Now we are going to build a microservice that interacts with others and is the front-facing façade to the customer.

When I was planning the contents of this chapter, a service like this one wasn't in it. However, after thinking about it, this chapter wouldn't have been the same without showing a few concepts around API aggregation that are fairly easy to show in a frontend microservice.

Need for frontend microservice

Think about scalability. When dealing with HTTP traffic, there is a pyramid of traffic. There are more hits in the frontend than in the backend. Usually, in order to reach the backend, the frontend needs to process the following few requests from the frontend:

- Read a form
- Validate it
- Manage the PRG pattern (https://en.wikipedia.org/wiki/Post/Redirect/Get)

As you can see, there is a lot of logic that needs to be processed by the frontend, so that it is not hard to see capacity problems if the software is busy. If we are using a microservice, and we are using it in the right way, scaling up or down should be an automatic process that can be triggered with a couple of clicks (or commands).

The code

Until now, we have pretty much always tested the code in a single server. This is fine for testing, but when we are building microservices, we want them to be distributed. Therefore, in order to achieve it, we need to indicate to Seneca how to reach the services:

```
var senecaEmailer = require("seneca")().client({
  host: "192.168.0.2",
  port: 8080
});
var senecaProductManager = require("seneca")().client({
  host: "192.168.0.3",
  port: 8080
});
var senecaOrderProcessor = require("seneca")().client({
  host: "192.168.0.4",
  port: 8080
});
```

What we have done is create three Seneca instances. They are like communication pipes between servers.

Let's explain the code:

Seneca, by default, uses the transport plugin TCP. It means that Seneca will be listening to the /act URL on the server. As an example, when we create senecaEmailer, the URL where Seneca will be pointing to is http://192.168.0.2:8080/act.

We can actually verify it with curl. If we execute the following command line, replacing <valid Seneca pattern> by a valid Seneca command, we should get a response from the server in the JSON format, which would be the second parameter in the done function for the action:

```
curl -d '<valid Seneca pattern>' -v http://192.168.0.2:8080/act
```

 Seneca's default transport plugin is TCP. If we don't specify any other, Seneca will use it to reach other servers and listen to calls.

Let's see an easy example:

```
var seneca = require("seneca")();
seneca.add({cmd: "test"}, function(args, done) {
  done(null, {response: "Hello World!"});
});

seneca.listen({port: 3000});
```

If we run this program, we can see the following output from the terminal:

```
2015-12-14T01:23:48.944Z asrwzxwx2u4e/1450920228931/7488/- INFO hello Seneca/0.8.0/asrwzxwx2u4e/1450920228931/7488/-
2015-12-14T01:23:49.102Z asrwzxwx2u4e/1450920228931/7488/- INFO listen {port:3000}
```

It means that Seneca is listening to the port 3000. Let's test it:

```
curl -d '{"cmd": "test"}' -v http://127.0.0.1:3000/act
```

This should print something very similar to the following code in the terminal:

```
*   Trying 127.0.0.1...
* Connected to 127.0.0.1 (127.0.0.1) port 3000 (#0)
> POST /act HTTP/1.1
> Host: 127.0.0.1:3000
> User-Agent: curl/7.43.0
> Accept: */*
> Content-Length: 15
> Content-Type: application/x-www-form-urlencoded
>
* upload completely sent off: 15 out of 15 bytes
< HTTP/1.1 200 OK
< Content-Type: application/json
< Cache-Control: private, max-age=0, no-cache, no-store
< Content-Length: 27
< seneca-id: i45q1ayb0wl1
< seneca-kind: res
< seneca-origin: curl/7.43.0
< seneca-accept: asrwzxwx2u4e/1450920228931/7488/-
< seneca-track:
< seneca-time-client-sent: 0
< seneca-time-listen-recv: 0
< seneca-time-listen-sent: 0
< Date: Thu, 14 Dec 2015 01:26:15 GMT
< Connection: keep-alive
<
* Connection #0 to host 127.0.0.1 left intact
{"response":"Hello World!"}%
```

The preceding code is the TCP/IP dialog between our terminal and Seneca server with the result of the response in the last line.

So, what we achieved earlier on having three different instances of Seneca is configuring our network of microservices; Seneca will transport the messages across the network for us.

The following flow diagram describes how a single API can hide multiple Seneca servers in the backend with different microservices (different Seneca instances, basically):

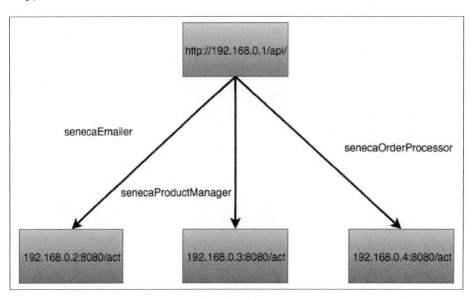

Now, let's take a look at the skeleton of the microservice:

```
var express = require("express");
var bodyParser = require('body-parser');
var senecaEmailer = require("seneca")().client({
  host: "192.168.0.2",
  port: 8080
});
var senecaProductManager = require("seneca")().client({
  host: "192.168.0.3",
  port: 8080
});
var senecaOrderProcessor = require("seneca")().client({
  host: "192.168.0.4",
  port: 8080
});

function api(options) {
  var seneca = this;

  /**
   * Gets the full list of products
```

```
  */
  seneca.add({area: "ui", action: "products"}, function(args,
    done) {
    // More code to come
  });
  /**
   * Get a product by id
   */
  seneca.add({area: "ui", action: "productbyid"}, function(args,
    done) {
    // More code to come
  });

  /**
   * Creates an order
   */
  seneca.add({area: "ui", action: "createorder"}, function(args,
    done) {
    // More code to come
  });

  this.add("init:api", function(msg, respond){
    seneca.act('role:web',{ use: {
      prefix: '/api',
      pin: 'area:ui,action:*',
      map: {
        products:  {GET:true}
        productbyid: {GET:true, suffix:'/:id'}
        createorder: {POST:true}
      }
    }}, respond)
  });
}
module.exports = api;
var seneca = require("seneca")();
seneca.use(api);

var app = require("express")();
app.use( require("body-parser").json());
app.use(seneca.export("web"));
app.listen(3000);
```

We have actually left the functionality that calls other microservices for later discussion. Now we are going to focus on how the code is articulated:

- We are creating a new plugin. The plugin is called `api` (the name of the function for wrapping the plugin is `api`).

- The plugin has to perform the following three actions:
    - List all the products
    - Get a product by ID
    - Create an order

- These three actions will call to two different microservices: Product Manager and Order Manager. We will come back to this topic later.

> Seneca can be seamlessly integrated with Express in order to provide web capabilities to Seneca microservices.

Until here, everything is well known, but what about the initialization function of the plugin?

At first look, it looks like dark magic:

```
this.add("init:api", function(msg, respond){
  seneca.act('role:web',{ use: {
    prefix: '/api',
    pin:   'area:ui,action:*',
    map: {
      products:   {GET:true}
      productbyid: {GET:true, suffix:'/:id'}
      createorder: {POST:true}
    }
  }}, respond)
});
```

Let's explain it:

1. Seneca will call the `init: <plugin-name>` action in order to initialize the plugin.

2. Through the `prefix` argument, we are listening to URLs under the `/api` path.

3. We are instructing Seneca to map the URLs to action by pinning a base common argument. In this case, all our `seneca.add(..)` contains an argument called `area` with the `ui` value. We are also asking Seneca to route calls that contain the `action` argument (no matter the value, that is why we use the *) so that it would ignore calls that don't specify the `action` argument.

The following argument (`map`) specifies the methods allowed in the matching.

How is the argument matching done?

The `area` argument is implicit as we have pinned it with the `ui` value.

The `action` argument needs to be present.

The URL must start with `/api` as we specified a prefix.

So, with this information, `/api/products` will correspond to the `{area: "ui", action: "products"}` action. In the same way, `/api/createorder` will correspond to the `{area: "ui", action:"createorder"}` action.

The `Productbyid` argument is a bit special.

> The Seneca `pin` keyword is used to assume that the calling code has a pair of argument-value so that it makes the code easier to understand, but be careful, implicit values can have bad effects to the readability.

Now, although it is not simple, this looks much easier.

Let's go back to the Seneca actions that are going to provide the functionality:

```
/**
 * Gets the full list of products.
 */
seneca.add({area: "ui", action: "products"}, function(args,
  done) {
  senecaProductManager.act({area: "product", action: "fetch"},
    function(err, result) {
    done(err, result);
  });
});

/**
 * Get a product by id.
 */
```

```
seneca.add({area: "ui", action: "productbyid"}, function(args,
    done) {
  senecaProductManager.act({area: "product", action: "fetch",
    criteria: "byId", id: args.id}, function(err, result) {
    done(err, result);
  });
});

/**
 * Creates an order to buy a single prodct.
 */
seneca.add({area: "ui", action: "createorder"}, function(args,
    done) {
  senecaProductManager.act({area: "product", action: "fetch",
    criteria: "byId", id: args.id}, function(err, product) {
    if(err) done(err, null);
    senecaOrderProcessor.act(area: "orders", action: "create",
      products: [product], email: args.email, name: args.name,
        function(err, order) {
      done(err, order);
    });
  });
});
```

 Warning! In the services written in this chapter, there is no data validation performed in order to make the concepts around the design of microservices clear. You should always validate the incoming data from untrusted systems (such as customers input).

We are actually using everything that we've discussed in the previous chapters, but we are taking a step forward in the Seneca semantics.

We have created an API with a very limited set of functionalities, but through them, we are aggregating the functionality of different microservices into one.

A detail to take into account is the amount of nested calls in the create order action (the last one). In this case, we are creating orders out of only a product to simplify the code, but if we are nesting too many calls for non-blocking actions waiting for the response in a callback, we will end up having a pyramid of code that makes your program difficult to read.

The solution for it would be to refactor how the data is fetched and/or reorganize the anonymous functions, avoiding inlining.

Another solution is the usage of promises libraries such as Q or Bluebird (`http://bluebirdjs.com/`) that allow us to chain the flow of the methods through promises:

```
myFunction().then(function() {
// Code here
}).then(function(){
// More code here
}).catch(function(error){
// Handle the error.
});
```

In this way, instead of building a sea of callbacks, we are nicely chaining the calls to the methods and adding error handlers to avoid the exceptions from bubbling up.

As you can see, we are using the UI as a central point of communication for all the microservices, except for the mailer, and we have a really good reason for it.

Service degradation – when the failure is not a disaster

Microservices are great, and we have demonstrated that by writing a small system in a few hundred lines of code that is fairly easy to understand.

They are also great as they allow us to react in the event of a failure:

- What happens if the e-mailer microservice stops working?
- What happens if the order processor stops working?
- Can we recover from the situation?
- What does the customer see?

These questions, on a monolithic system, are nonsense. The e-mailer probably would be a part of the application. The failure on sending an e-mail implies a general error, unless it is specifically handled. Same with the order processor.

However, what about our microservices-oriented architecture?

The fact that the e-mailer has failed to deliver a few e-mails does not prevent the orders from being processed, even though the customers aren't getting the e-mails. This is what we call performance or service degradation; the system might be slower, but some functionalities will still work.

Service degradation is the ability of a system to lose a feature without suffering a general failure.

What about the order manager? Well...we can still make the products-related calls work, but we won't be able to process any order...which might still be a good thing.

The fact that the order manager is responsible for sending the e-mail instead of the UI microservice is not coincidental; we only want to send the e-mail with the acknowledgement of a sale on the success event, and we don't want to send the success e-mail in any other case.

Circuit breakers

In the previous section, we talked about system degradation in the event of a failure, but everybody who has worked in IT for a number of years knows that a system does not fail suddenly in most cases of failures.

The most common event is a timeout; the server is busy for a period of time, which makes the request to fail, giving our customers a terrible user experience.

How can we solve this particular problem?

We can solve this problem with a circuit breaker, as shown in the following image:

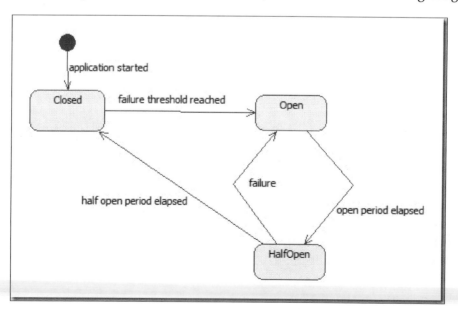

A circuit breaker is a mechanism to prevent requests from reaching an unstable server that could cause our application to misbehave.

As you can see in the preceding schema, the circuit breaker has the following three statuses:

- **Closed**: The circuit is closed; the requests reach their destination.
- **Open**: The circuit is open; the requests don't get past the circuit breaker and the client gets an error. The system will retry the communication after a time period.
- **HalfOpen**: The circuit tests the service again, and if there is no error reaching it, the requests can flow again and the circuit breaker is **Closed**.

With this simple mechanism, we can prevent the errors to cascade through our system, avoiding catastrophic failures.

Ideally, the circuit breaker should be asynchronous. This means that even if there are no requests, every few seconds/milliseconds, the system should be trying to re-establish the connection to the faulty service in order to continue the normal operation.

 Failure is a common denominator in the human nature: better be prepared for it.

Circuit breakers are also an ideal place to alert the support engineers. Depending on the nature of our system, the fact that a given service cannot be reached could mean a serious issue. Can you imagine a bank that is unable to reach the SMS service to send two-factor authentication codes? No matter how hard we try, it will always happen at some point. So, be prepared for it.

 There is a very inspiring article from Martin Fowler (one of the big names in microservices) about circuit breakers at http://martinfowler. com/bliki/CircuitBreaker.html.

Seneca – a simple puzzle that makes our lives easier

Seneca is great. It enables the developers to take a simple and small idea and translate it into a piece of code with a connection point that does not make any assumption, just facts. An action has a clear input and provides you the interface to give an answer for it through a callback.

How many times have you found your team struggling with the class structure of an application just to reuse code in *a nice way*?

Seneca focuses on **simplicity**. The fact that we are not modeling objects, but just parts of systems using small portions of code that are extremely cohesive and idempotent to objects makes our life much easier.

Another way how Seneca makes our life easy is through the **plugability**.

If you review the code that we have been writing in this book, the first thing that will be spotted is how convenient the plugins are.

They provide the right level of encapsulation for a bunch of actions (Does it look similar to a class?) that are somehow related to each other.

I always try not to over-engineer solutions. It is really easy to fall into premature abstraction, preparing the code for a future that we don't know whether it it is going to happen in the majority of the cases.

We don't realize how long we spend maintaining features that have been overdesigned and need to be tested every time someone changes the code around them.

Seneca avoids (or at least discourages) this type of designs. Think about Seneca actions as a small piece of paper (like a post-it), where you need to write what happened last week. You need to be smart about what to fit in there, and possibly, split it into another post-it if the content gets to dense.

Another point where Seneca is good is in configurability. As we have seen before, Seneca comes with a number of integrations for data storage and transport.

An important side of Seneca is the transport protocol. As we know by now, the default transport is carried over TCP, but can we use a message queue to do it? The structure is shown as follows:

Yes, we can. It is already done and maintained.

 The following URL is a plugin for Seneca that allows it to send messages over RabbitMQ instead of HTTP:

`https://github.com/senecajs/seneca-rabbitmq-transport`

If you look into the code of the plugin (it looks really complex, but it is not), you can spot where the magic happens in few seconds:

```
    seneca.add({role: 'transport', hook: 'listen', type: 'rabbitmq'},
  hook_listen_rabbitmq)
    seneca.add({role: 'transport', hook: 'client', type: 'rabbitmq'},
  hook_client_rabbitmq)
```

Seneca is using Seneca actions to delegate the transport of the message. Although it looks a bit recursive, it is brilliant!

Once you understand how Seneca and the transport protocol chosen work, you are immediately qualified to write a transport plugin for Seneca.

 When I started learning about Seneca in order to write this book, I also wrote a transport plugin to use NServiceBus (`http://particular.net/`).

NServiceBus is an interesting idea, it allows you to connect a number of storages and AMPQ-compliant systems and use them as clients. For example, we could be writing messages in a SQL Server table and consuming them from a queue once they get routed through NServiceBus, having immediate auditing capabilities on the history of the messages.

With such flexibility, we could potentially write a plugin that uses pretty much anything as a transport protocol.

Seneca and promises

All our code from the previous chapters is relying on callbacks. Callbacks are good as far as your code does not nest them on more than three levels.

However, there is an even better way of managing the asynchronous nature of JavaScript: **promises**.

Take a look at the following code:

```
<!doctype html>
<html lang="en">
<head>
  <meta charset="utf-8">
  <title>promise demo</title>
<script src="https://code.jquery.com/jquery-1.10.2.js"></script>
</head>
<body>

<button>Go</button>
<p>Ready...</p>
<div></div>
<div></div>
<div></div>
<div></div>

<script>
var effect = function() {
  return $( "div" ).fadeIn( 800 ).delay( 1200 ).fadeOut();
};

$( "button" ).on( "click", function() {
  $( "p" ).append( " Started... " );

  $.when( effect() ).done(function() {
  $( "p" ).append( " Finished! " );
  });
});
</script>

</body>
</html>
```

The preceding code is an example of the JQuery fragment using promises.

A promise, by its definition is:

A declaration or assurance that one will do something or that a particular thing will happen.

That is exactly it. If you see the preceding code, $.when, returns a promise. We don't know how long the effect function will take, but we can guarantee that once it is ready, the function inside of done will be executed. It looks very similar to callbacks, but take a look at the following code:

```
callhttp(url1, data1).then(function(result1) {
    // result1 is available here
    return callhttp(url2, data2);
}).then(function(result2) {
    // only result2 is available here
    return callhttp(url3, data3);
}).then(function(result3) {
    // all three are done now, final result is in result3
});
```

Don't try to execute it, it is just a hypothetical example, but what we are doing in there is chain promises; and that makes the code vertical instead of ending up in a pyramid-shaped program, which is a lot harder to read, as shown in the following diagram:

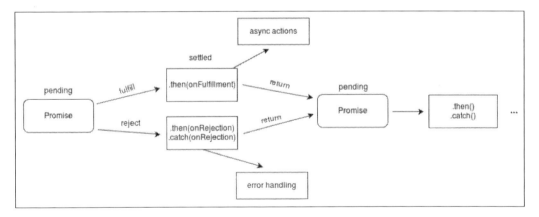

Seneca, by default, is not a promise-oriented framework, but (there is always a but) using Bluebird, one of the most famous promises libraries in JavaScript, we can *promisify* Seneca, as follows:

```
var Promise = require('bluebird');
var seneca = require('seneca')();

// Promisify the .act() method; to learn more about this technique
  see:
// http://bluebirdjs.com/docs/features.html#promisification-on-
  steroids
var act = Promise.promisify(seneca.act, seneca);

// Return no error and a success message to illustrate a resolved
  promise
seneca.add({cmd: 'resolve'}, function (args, done) {
  done(null, {message: "Yay, I've been resolved!"});
});

// Return an error to force a rejected promise
seneca.add({cmd: 'reject'}, function (args, done) {
  done(new Error("D'oh! I've been rejected."));
});

// Use the new promisified act() with no callback
act({cmd: 'resolve'})
  .then(function (result) {
  // result will be {message: "Yay, I've been resolved!"} since
  // its guaranteed to resolve
  })
  .catch(function (err) {
  // Catch any error as usual if it was rejected
  });

act({cmd: 'reject'})
  .then(function (result) {
  // Never reaches here since we throw an error on purpose
  })
  .catch(function (err) {
  // err will be set with message "D'oh! I've been rejected."
  });
```

There are two important details in the preceding code:

```
var act = Promise.promisify(seneca.act, seneca);
```

This creates a promisified version of the `act` function and its use, as follows:

```
act({cmd: 'reject'})
  .then(function (result) {
  // Never reaches here since we throw an error on purpose
  })
  .catch(function (err) {
  // err will be set with message "D'oh! I've been rejected."
  });
```

An important detail in this last fragment; instead of receiving a callback with the following two parameters:

- An error
- The results

We are chaining the following two methods:

- **Then**: This is executed when the promise is resolved
- **Catch**: This is executed if there is an error while resolving the promise

This type of constructions allows us to write the following code:

```
act({cmd: 'timeout'})
  .then(function (result) {
  // Never reaches here since the gate executer times out
  })
  .catch(function (err) {
  // err will be set with a timeout error thrown by the gate executer
  });
```

This code is handling something that we have never talked about before: the gate executor timeouts. It happens when Seneca cannot reach the destination in some situations, and it can be easily handled with a promise as shown earlier. The `then` part would never be executed as the function will only be called when there is an error.

There are a few well-consolidated options in the market now for promises in JavaScript. Nowadays, my preferred choice would be Bluebird (`https://github.com/petkaantonov/bluebird`) because of its simplicity. Q is another option used by AngularJS (one of the most popular **SPA** frameworks), but for day-to-day use, it looks more complicated than Bluebird.

Debugging

Debugging a Node.js application is very similar to debugging any other application. IDEs like **WebStorm** or **IntelliJ** provide a traditional debugger where you can install breakpoints and stop the execution whenever the application hits the given line.

This is perfect if you buy a license for one of the IDEs, but there is a free alternative that will have a very similiar result for the users of Google Chrome, **node-inspector**.

Node-inspector is an npm package that pretty much enables the Chrome debugger to debug Node.js applications.

Let's see how it works:

1. First of all, we need to install node-inspector:

   ```
   npm install -g node-inspector
   ```

   This should add a command to our system called node-inspector. If we execute it, we get the following output:

   ```
   ➜ code node-inspector
   Node Inspector v0.12.7
   Visit http://127.0.0.1:8080/?port=5858 to start debugging.
   ```

   That means our debug server has started.

2. Now we need to run a node application with a special flag to indicate that it needs to be debugged.

   Let's take a simple Seneca act as an example:

   ```
   var seneca = require( 'seneca' )()
   seneca.add({role: 'math', cmd: 'sum'}, function (msg,
     respond) {
     var sum = msg.left + msg.right
     respond(null, {answer: sum})
   })

   seneca.add({role: 'math', cmd: 'product'}, function (msg,
     respond) {
     var product = msg.left * msg.right
     respond( null, { answer: product } )
   })

   seneca.act({role: 'math', cmd: 'sum', left: 1, right: 2},
     console.log)
   ```

```
seneca.act({role: 'math', cmd: 'product', left: 3, right: 4},
    console.log)
```

3. Now, in order to run it on the debug mode, execute the following command:

    ```
    node index.js --debug-brk
    ```

    The way to access the debugger is through the URL http://127.0.0.1:808
    0/?port=5858:

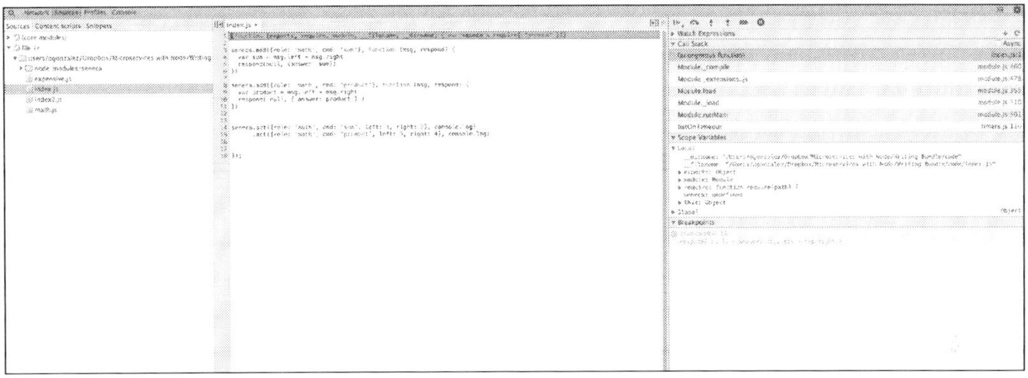

I am sure this image is very familiar to every developer in the world: it is the Chrome
debugger showing our code. As you can see in the first line, the one highlighted
in blue, the application stopped in the first instruction so that we can place the
breakpoints by clicking the line numbers, as shown in the following image:

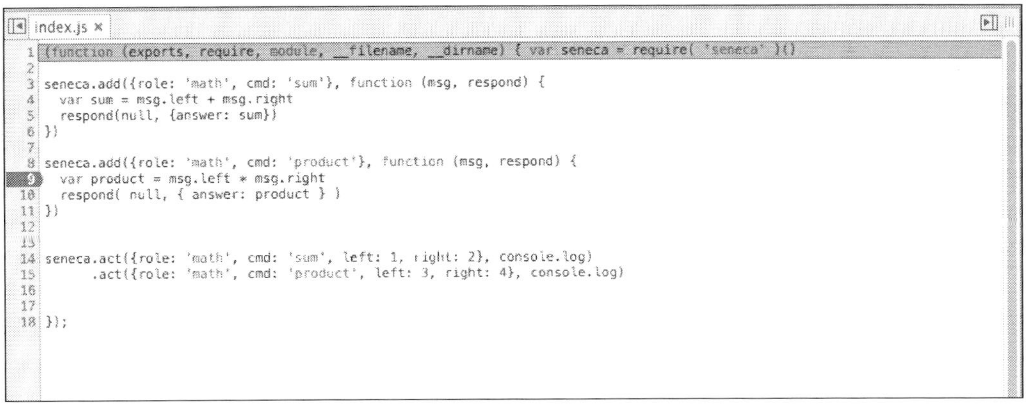

As you can see in the preceding image, we have installed a breakpoint in line **9**. Now we can use the control panel to navigate through the code and values of our variables:

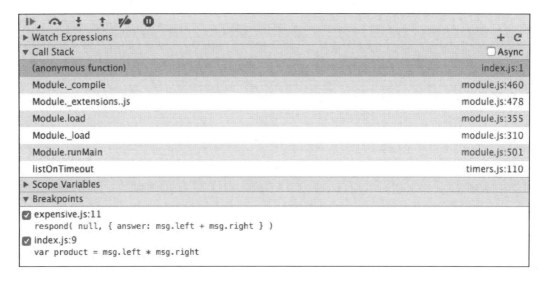

The controls on the top speak for themselves if you ever debugged an application:

- The first button is called play and it allows the application to run to the next breakpoint

- Step over executes the next line in the current file

- Step into goes into the next line, getting deeper in the call stack so that we can see the call hierarchy

- Step out is the reverse of step into

- Disable breakpoints will prevent the program from stopping at the breakpoints

- Pause on exceptions, as its name indicates, will cause the program to stop on exceptions (it is very useful when trying to catch errors)

If we click on play, we can see how the script will stop in line **9** in the following image:

```
index.js ×

1 (function (exports, require, module, __filename, __dirname) { var seneca = require( 'seneca' )()
2
3 seneca.add({role: 'math', cmd: 'sum'}, function (msg, respond) {
4   var sum = msg.left + msg.right
5   respond(null, {answer: sum})
6 })
7
8 seneca.add({role: 'math', cmd: 'product'}, function (msg, respond) {
9   var product = msg.left * msg.right
10   respond( null, { answer: product } )
11 })
12
13                Object
14 seneca.act({        cmd: "product"                    sole.log)
15        .act({       default$: undefined               console.log)
16                      left: 3
17                    ▶ meta$: Object
18 });                  right: 4
                        role: "math"
                        tx$: "v36m52ndnt10"
                     ▶ __proto__: Object
```

As a good debugger, it will let us inspect the value of our variables by hovering the cursor over the variable name.

Summary

This chapter has been pretty intense. We have gone through a lot of content that helped us in building a small microservices ecosystem that, when orchestrated together, would fairly work well. We have been a bit simplistic some times, but the idea of the book is to indicate the power of the microservices-oriented software. At this stage, I would recommend the reader to start performing some testing around Seneca.

The documentation on the website is quite helpful, and there are a lot of examples to follow.

There are a few plugins for storage and transport, as well as other type of plugins (such as user authentication), that would allow you to experiment with different features of Seneca.

We will be talking more about some of them in the following chapters.

5
Security and Traceability

Security is one of the biggest concerns in systems nowadays. The amount of information leaked from big companies is worrying, especially because 90% of the information leaks could be mended with very small actions by the software developers. Something similar happens with the logging of events and the traceability of errors. No one really pays too much attention until someone requests the logs that you don't have in order to audit a failure. In this chapter, we will discuss how to manage security and logging so that our system is safe and traceable, with the help of the following topics:

- **Infrastructure logical security**: We will discuss how to secure our software infrastructure in order to provide the industry standard security layer in our communications.

- **Application security**: We will introduce the common techniques to secure our applications. Practices such as output encoding or input validation are the industry standard and they could save us from a catastrophe.

- **Traceability**: Being able to follow the requests around our system is a must in microservices architectures. We will leverage this task to Seneca and learn how to get the information from this fantastic framework.

- **Auditing**: Even though we put our best efforts in building a software, accidents happen. The ability to rebuild the sequence of calls and see exactly what happened is important. We will discuss how to enable our system in order to be able to recover the required information.

Infrastructure logical security

Infrastructure security is usually ignored by software engineers as it is completely different from their area of expertise. However, nowadays, and especially if your career is leaning towards DevOps, it is a subject that should not be ignored.

In this book, we are not going to go very deep into the infrastructure security more than few rules of thumb to keep your microservices safe.

It is strongly recommended for the readers to read and learn about cryptography and all the implications around the usage of SSH, which is one of the main resources for keeping communications secure nowadays.

SSH – encrypting the communications

In any organization, there is a strict list of people who can access certain services. In general, this authentication for these services is done via username and password, but it can also be done using a key to *verify the identity of the user*.

No matter what authentication method is used, the communication should always be done over a secure channel such as **SSH**.

SSH stands for **Secure Shell** and it is a software used to access shells in remote machines, but it can also be a very helpful tool to create proxies and tunnels to access remote servers.

Let's explain how it works using the following command:

```
/home/david:(develop) × ssh david@192.168.0.1
The authenticity of host '192.168.0.1 (192.168.0.1)' can't be
established.
RSA key fingerprint is SHA256:S22/A2/
eqxSqkS4VfR1BrcDxNX1rmfM1JkZaGhrjMbk.
Are you sure you want to continue connecting (yes/no)? yes
Warning: Permanently added '192.168.0.1' (RSA) to the list of known
hosts.
vagrant@192.168.0.1's password:
Last login: Mon Jan 25 02:30:21 2016 from 10.0.2.2
Welcome to your virtual machine.
```

In this case, I am using **Vagrant** to facilitate the building of virtual machines. Vagrant is a very popular tool to automate development environments and their website (https://www.vagrantup.com/) consists of useful information.

In the first line, we execute the `ssh david@192.168.0.1` command. This command tries to open a terminal as the user `david` in the `192.168.0.1` host.

As it is the first time that this command is executed against the machine in the IP `192.168.0.1`, our computer will not trust the remote server.

This is done by maintaining a file called `known_hosts`, under the `/home/david/.ssh/known_hosts` folder in this case (it will depend on the user).

This file is a list of hosts with the corresponding key. As you can see, the following two lines explain that the *host cannot be trusted* and present the fingerprint of the key held by the remote server in order to verify it:

```
The authenticity of host '192.168.0.1 (192.168.0.1)' can't be
established.
RSA key fingerprint is SHA256:S22/A2/
eqxSqkS4VfR1BrcDxNX1rmfM1JkZaGhrjMbk.
```

At this point, the user is supposed to verify the identity of the server by checking the key. Once this is done, we can instruct SSH to connect to the server, which will result in the following log being printed:

```
Warning: Permanently added '192.168.0.1' (RSA) to the list of known
hosts.
```

Now, if we check our `known_hosts` file, we can see that the key has been added to the list, as follows:

```
192.168.0.1 ssh-rsa AAAAB3NzaC1yc2EAAAABIwAAAQEAxO/9E+joR8X46RLZV/wbcC15+qmQGPjfXsfpn97GV
OazzNgndR16t6WSxXmUR71fbEsjeZRYdhGp4ckkDh8AZ01MbNPuP6cKWHqy0LtOxXQR5hF/unShU8pwOPPJn8RxPB
ia3SLQ3BskfNxOrUijGqKs1JuRfeQafPuHvs0Q2kJH8PYD2UyEreHuLWiEuaiQuIguG8UiNEUkuIJEAyhD+PGVMLV
khhlTMZ+Pl0BhK7Q/9kF1e8D/ws2iBIB6I3oQx/FGW2dXuLbox0DPX7iRgazf8YRv2lIWkKrh+qoD7sjTVCUgMMd4
1TbPIkNf3yrkDUQaRrfdWF0KXQ8JbNuKGhvgw==
```

This key stored in the `known_hosts` file is the public key of the remote server.

SSH uses a **cryptography algorithm** called **RSA**. This algorithm is built around the concept of **asymmetric cryptography**, which is shown in the following image:

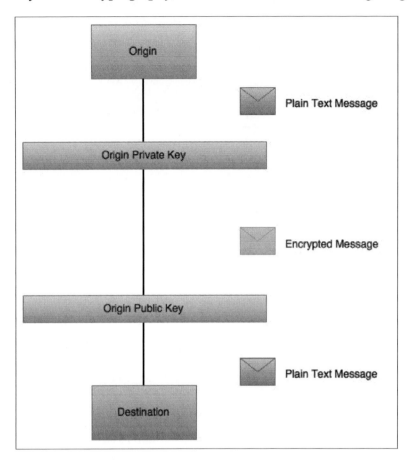

The asymmetric cryptography relies on a set of keys: one public and one private. As the name states, the public key can be shared with everyone; whereas, the private key has to be kept secret.

The messages encrypted with the private key can only be decrypted with the public key and the other way around so that it is almost impossible (unless someone gets the other half of the key) to intercept and decrypt a message.

At this point, our computer knows the public key of the server and we are in a position to start an encrypted session with the server. Once we get the terminal, all the commands and results of these commands will be encrypted and sent over the wire.

This key can also be used to connect to a remote server without password. The only thing we need to do is generate an SSH key in our machine and install it in the server in a file called `authorized_keys` under the `.ssh` folder, where the `known_hosts` file is.

When working with microservices, you can be remotely logged in to quite a few different machines so that this approach becomes more attractive. However, we need to be very careful about how we handle the private keys because if a user leaks that private key, our infrastructure could be compromised.

Application security

Application security is becoming more and more important. As the cloud is becoming the de-facto standard for infrastructure in large companies, we can't rely on the fact that the data is confined in a single data centre.

Usually, when someone starts a new business, the main focus is to build the product from the functional point of view. Security is not the main focus and usually gets overlooked.

This is a very dangerous practice and we are going to amend that by letting the reader know the main security threats that could compromise our application.

The main four big security points to develop applications in a secure manner are as follows:

- Injection
- Cross-site scripting
- Cross-site request forgery token protection
- Open redirects

At the end of this section, we will be able to identify the main vulnerabilities, but we won't be armored against a malicious attacker. In general, a software engineer should be up to date with the security as much as they are up to date with new technologies. No matter how good the product you build is, if it is not secure, someone will find out and take the advantage of it.

Common threats – how to be up to date

As we stated before, security is an ongoing subject in application development. No matter what type of software you are building, there will always be security implications around it.

The best way I've found during my professional career to be up to date with security around web development without being a full-time dedicated security engineer is to follow the **OWASP** project. **OWASP** stands for **Open Web Application Security Project** and they produce quite an interesting document (among others) on a yearly basis called OWASP Top 10.

 OWASP Top 10 was first published in 2003 and its goal is to raise awareness in the development community about the most common threats in application development.

In the previous section, we identified the four main security issues that a software developer can face and all of them are mentioned in the following sections.

Injection

Injection is, by far, the most dangerous attack that we could be exposed to. Specifically, a SQL injection is the most common form of injection that affects applications and it consists of an attacker forcing a SQL code in one of our application queries, leading to a different query that could compromise the data of our company.

There are other types of injections, but we are going to focus on SQL injection, as pretty much every application in the modern world uses a relational database.

SQL injection consists of the injection or manipulation of SQL queries in our application through the input from non-validated sources, such as a web form or any other data source with arbitrary input of text.

Let's consider the following example:

```
SELECT * FROM users WHERE username = 'username' AND password = 'password'
```

 Never store passwords in plain in the database. Always hash and salt them to avoid rainbow-table attacks. This is just an example.

This query will give us the user that corresponds to a given name and password. In order to build the query from the client's input, we can consider doing something similar to the following code as a good idea:

```
var express = require('express');
var app = express();
var mysql      = require('mysql');

var connection = mysql.createConnection({
```

```
  host     : 'localhost',
  user     : 'me',
  password : 'secret',
  database : 'test_db'
});

app.get('/login', function(req, res) {
  var username = req.param("username");
  var password = req.param("password");

  connection.connect();
  var query = "SELECT * FROM users WHERE username = '" + username
    + "' AND password = '" + password + "'";
  connection.query(query, function(err, rows, fields) {
    if (err) throw err;
    res.send(rows);
  });
  connection.end();
});

app.listen(3000, function() {
  console.log("Application running in port 3000.");
});
```

At first sight, it looks like an easy program that accesses the database called `test_db` and issues a query to check whether there is a user that matches the username and password and renders it back to the client so that if we open the browser and try to browse to the `http://localhost:3000/login?username=david&password=mypassw ord` URL, the browser will render a JSON object with the result of the following query:

`SELECT * FROM users WHERE username = 'david' AND password = 'mypassword'`

Nothing strange yet, but what happens if the customer tries to hack us?

Take a look at the following input:

`http://localhost:3000/login?username=' OR 1=1 --&password=mypassword`

As you can see, the query generated by it is the following code:

`SELECT * FROM users WHERE username = '' OR 1=1 -- AND password = 'mypassword'`

In SQL, the `--` character sequence is used to comment the rest of the line so that the effective query would be as follows:

`SELECT * FROM users WHERE username='' OR 1=1`

This query returns the full list of users, and if our software is using the result of this query to resolve whether the user should be logged in or not, we are in some serious problems. We have just granted access to our system to someone who does not even know a valid username.

This is one of the many examples on how SQL injection can affect us.

In this case, it is pretty obvious that we are concatenating untrusted data (coming from the user) into our query, but believe me, when the software gets more complicated, it is not always easy to identify.

A way to avoid SQL injection is through the usage of prepared statements.

Input validation

Applications interact with users mainly through forms. These forms usually contain free text input fields that could lead to an attack.

The easiest way to prevent corrupted data from getting into our server is through input validation, which as the name suggests, consists of validating the input from the user to avoid the situation described earlier.

There are two types of input validation, as follows:

- White listing
- Black listing

Black listing is a dangerous technique. In majority of cases, trying to define what is incorrect in the input takes a lot more effort than simply defining what we expect.

The recommended approach is (and will always be) to **white list** the data coming from the user, validating it through the use of a regular expression: we know how a phone number looks like, we also know how a username should look like, and so on.

Input validation is not always easy. If you have ever come across the validation of an e-mail, you will know what I am talking about: the regular expression to validate an e-mail is anything but simple.

The fact that there is not an easy way to validate some data should not restrict us from doing it as the omission of input validation could lead to a serious security flaw.

Input validation is not the silver bullet for SQL injections, but it also helps with other security threats such as cross-site scripting.

In the query from the previous section, we do something quite dangerous: concatenate user input into our query.

One of the solutions could be to use some sort of escaping library that will sanitize the input from the user, as follows:

```
app.get('/login', function(req, res) {
    var username = req.param("username");
    var password = req.param("password");

    connection.connect();
    var query = "SELECT * FROM users WHERE username = '" +
        connection.escape(username) + "' AND password = '" +
        connection.escape(password) + "'";
    connection.query(query, function(err, rows, fields) {
        if (err) throw err;
        res.send(rows);
    });
    connection.end();
});
```

In this case, the `mysql` library used provides a suite of methods to escape strings. Let's see how it works:

```
var mysql = require('mysql');
var connection = mysql.createConnection({
    host: 'localhost',
    username: 'root',
    password: 'root'
});

console.log(connection.escape("' OR 1=1 --"))
```

The small script from earlier escapes the string provided as `username` in the previous example, the result is `\' OR 1=1 --`.

As you can see, the `escape()` method has replaced the dangerous characters, sanitizing the input from the user.

Cross-site scripting

Cross-site scripting, also known as **XSS**, is a security vulnerability that mainly affects web applications. It is one of the most common security issues and the implications can be huge for the customer as potentially, someone could steal the user identity with this attack.

The attack is an injection code put into a third-party website that could steal data from the client's browser. There are a few ways of doing it, but by far, the most common is by unescaped input from the client.

In few websites on the Internet, users can add comments containing arbitrary input. This arbitrary input can contain script tags that load a JavaScript from a remote server that can steal the session cookie (or other types of valuable information), letting the attacker replicate the user session on a remote machine.

There are two main types of XSS attacks: **persistent** and **non-persistent**.

The **persistent** type of XSS consists of storing the XSS attack by crafting a particular string of text that resolves into the attack once it is displayed to the user in the website. This code could be injected via an arbitrary input text that is stored in the database (such as a comment in a forum).

The **non-persistent** type of XSS is when the attack is inserted into a non-persistent part of the application due to bad data handling.

Let's take a look at the following screenshot:

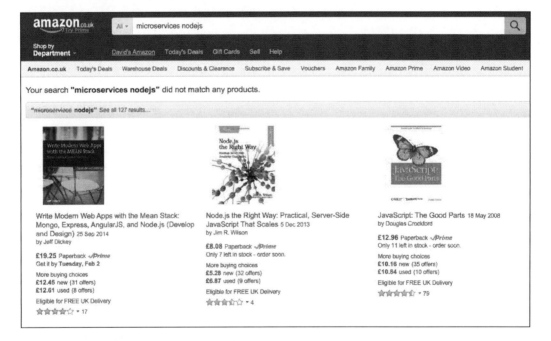

As you can see, we have searched for a book (this book) in `http://www.amazon.co.uk/`. It does not produce any output (as the book is not published yet), but it specifies that **Your search "microservices nodejs" did not match any products**, which is somehow using the input from the web browser as output. Even more, when I clicked on search, Amazon redirected me to the following URL:

```
http://www.amazon.co.uk/s/ref=nb_sb_noss?url=search-
alias%3Daps&field-keywords=microservices+nodejs
```

We know Amazon is secure, but if it was sensible to XSS attacks, we could have modified the value of the `field-keywords` parameter to craft a request that injected a script tag in the content, leading to the attacker being able to steal the session cookie that could result in some serious problems for the website.

Output encoding

A way to protect against this attack is output encoding. We have done it before, when we used `connection.escape()` in the *Input validation* section of this chapter. In fairness, we should be validating all the data entered from the user and encoding all the outputs that come from third parties. This includes the input entered by the user, as well as sources of information coming from outside of the system.

When narrowing the problem to web development, we have to be aware of the three different areas where output encoding is needed:

- CSS
- JavaScript
- HTML

The most problematic two are JavaScript and HTML, where an attacker could easily steal information without too much effort.

Generally, no matter which framework we use for building our app, it always has functions to encode the output.

Cross-site request forgery

Cross-site request forgery (**CSRF**) is the reverse of cross-site request scripting. In cross-site request scripting, the problem is in the client trusting the data coming from the server. With cross-site request forgery, the problem is that the server trusts the data coming from the client.

After stealing the session cookie, the attacker can not only steal information from the user, but can also modify the information of the account associated with the cookie.

This is done by posting the data to the server via HTTP requests.

HTTP classifies its requests in methods. A method is basically used to specify what is the operation to be carried by the request. The most interesting four methods are the following ones:

- GET: This gets the data from the server. It should not modify any persistent data.
- POST: This creates a resource in the server.
- PUT: This updates a resource in the server.
- DELETE: This deletes a resource from the server.

There are more methods (such as PATCH or CONNECT), but let's focus on these four. As you can see, three of these four methods modify data from the server, and a user with a valid session could potentially steal data, create payments, order goods, and so on.

A way to avoid the cross-site request forgery attack is by protecting the POST, PUT and DELETE endpoints with a cross-site request token.

Take a look at the following HTML form:

```
<form action="/register" method="post">
  <input name="email" type="text" />
  <input name="password" type="password" />
</form>
```

This form describes a perfectly valid situation: a user registering on our website; very simple, but still valid and flawed.

We are specifying a URL and the list of expected parameters so that an attacker can register hundreds or thousands of accounts within a span of minutes, with a small script that issues a POST request with the two parameters (email and password) in the body.

Now, look at the following form:

```
<form action="/register" method="post">
  <input name="email" type="text" />
  <input name="password" type="password" />
  <input name="csrftoken" type="hidden"
    value="as7d6fasd678f5a5sf5asf" />
</form>
```

You can see the difference: there is an extra hidden parameter called csrftoken.

This parameter is a random string that is generated every time a form is rendered so that we can add this extra parameter to every form.

Once the form is submitted, the `csrftoken` parameter is validated to only let go through the requests with a valid token and generate a new token to be rendered on the page again.

Open redirects

Sometimes, our application might need to redirect the user to a certain URL. For example, when hitting a private URL without a valid authentication, the user will usually be redirected to the login page:

```
http://www.mysite.com/my-private-page
```

This could result into a redirect to the following:

```
http://www.mysite.com/login?redirect=/my-private-page
```

This sounds legit. The user is sent to the login page, and once he provides a valid set of credentials, it is redirected to `/my-private-page`.

What happens if someone tries to steal the account of our user?

Look at the following request:

```
http://www.mysite.com/login?redirect=http://myslte.com
```

This is a crafted request that will redirect the user to `myslte.com` instead of `mysite.com` (note the `l` instead of `i`).

Someone could make `myslte.com` look like the login page of `mysite.com` and steal your user's password and username by distributing the preceding URL in the social media as the users will be redirected to a malicious page.

The solution for the preceding problem is quite simple: don't redirect the user to untrusted third-party websites.

Again, the best way of doing such task is white listing the target hosts for redirects. Basically, we don't let our software redirect our customers to unknown websites.

Effective code reviews

One of the most effective ways to reduce security flaws in our applications is through a systematic and informed code review process. The problem with code reviews is that they always end up being a dump area for opinions and personal preferences that usually not only won't improve the quality of the code, but will also lead to last minute changes that could expose vulnerabilities in our application.

A dedicated stage in the product development life cycle for a security code review helps to drastically reduce the amount of bugs delivered to production.

The problem that the software engineers have is that their mind is trained to build things that work well, but they don't have the mindset to find defects, especially around the things that they build. This is why you should not be testing your own code (any further than the test carried on when developing), and even less, security testing your application.

However, we usually work in teams and that enables us to review someone else's code, but we have to do it in an effective manner.

Code reviews require as much brain power as needed to write software, especially if you are reviewing a complex code. You should never spend more than two hours reviewing the same functionality, otherwise important flaws will be missed and attention to detail will decrease to a worrying level.

This is not a big problem in microservices-based architectures as the functionality should be small enough to be read in a reasonable period of time, especially if you talked to the author about what he was trying to build.

You should always follow a two phase review, as follows:

- Review the code quickly to get the big picture: how it works, what technology it uses that you are not familiar with, does it do what it is supposed to do, and so on
- Review the code following a checklist of items to look for

This list of items has to be decided upfront and depends on the nature of the software that your company is building.

Usually, the list of items to check around the code security concerns during a code review is quite big, but we can narrow it down to the following components:

- Is all the input validated/encoded when applicable?
- Is all the output encoded, including logs?
- Do we protect endpoints with cross-site request forgery tokens?
- Are all the user credentials encrypted or hashed in the database?

If we check this list, we will be able to identify the biggest issues around security in our apps.

Traceability

Traceability is extremely important in the modern information systems. It is a delicate matter in microservices that is gracefully solved in Seneca, making the requests easy to follow around our system so that we can audit the failure.

Logging

Seneca is pretty good with the logging. There are so many options that can be configured in Seneca in order to get the required information about how everything is working (if it is working).

Let's see how logging works with a small application:

```
var seneca = require("seneca")();

seneca.add({cmd: "greeter"}, function(args, callback){
  callback(null, {message: "Hello " + args.name});
});

seneca.act({cmd: "greeter", name: "David"}, function(err, result) {
  console.log(result);
});
```

This is the simplest Seneca application that can be written. Let's run it as follows:

```
seneca  node index.js
2016-02-01T09:55:40.962Z 3rhomq69cbe0/1454579740947/84217/- INFO hello Se
neca/1.0.0/3rhomq69cbe0/1454579740947/84217/-
{ message: 'Hello David' }
```

This is the result of running the app with the default logging configuration. Aside from the `console.log()` method that we have used in the code, there is some internal information about Seneca being logged. Sometimes, you might want to only log what your application is producing so that you can debug the application without all the noise. In this case, just run the following command:

```
seneca  node index.js --seneca.log.quiet
{ message: 'Hello David' }
```

However, sometimes, there are weird behaviors in the system (or even a bug in the frameworks used) and you want to get all the information about what is happening. Seneca supports that as well, as shown in the following command:

```
seneca  node index.js --seneca.log.print
```

The preceding command will print an endless amount of information that might not be helpful.

In order to reduce the amount of logging produced by Seneca, there is a fine-grain control in what gets logged into the output. Let's take a look at the following lines:

```
2016-02-01T10:00:07.191Z dyy9ixcavqu4/1454580006885/85010/- DEBUG
register install transport {exports:[transport/utils]} seneca-8t1dup
```

```
2016-02-01T10:00:07.305Z dyy9ixcavqu4/1454580006885/85010/- DEBUG
register init seneca-y9os9j
```

```
2016-02-01T10:00:07.305Z dyy9ixcavqu4/1454580006885/85010/- DEBUG plugin
seneca-y9os9j DEFINE {}
```

```
2016-02-01T10:00:07.330Z dyy9ixcavqu4/1454580006885/85010/-
DEBUG act root$      IN o5onzziv9i7a/b7dtf6v1u9sq cmd:greeter
{cmd:greeter,name:David} ENTRY (mnb89) - - -
```

They are random lines from a log output on the preceding code example, but it will give us useful information: these entries are debug-level log lines for different actions (such as plugin, register, and act) on the Seneca framework. In order to filter them, Seneca provides a control over what levels or actions do we want to see. Consider the following for example:

```
node index.js --seneca.log=level:INFO
```

This will only output the logs related to the INFO level:

```
seneca  node index.js --seneca.log=level:INFO
2016-02-04T10:39:04.685Z q6wnh8qmm113/1454582344670/91823/- INFO hello
Seneca/1.0.0/q6wnh8qmm113/1454582344670/91823/-
{ message: 'Hello David' }
```

You can also filter by action type, which is quite interesting. When you are working with microservices, knowing the chain of events that happened in a flow is one of the first things that you need to look into in order to audit a failure. With this control over the logging that Seneca gives us, it is as easy as executing the following command:

```
node index.js --seneca.log=type:act
```

This will produce the following output:

As you can see, all the preceding lines correspond to the `act` type, and even more, if we follow the output of the command from top to bottom, we exactly know the sequence of events to which Seneca reacted and their order.

Tracing requests

Tracing requests is also a very important activity, and sometimes, it is even a legal requirement, especially if you work in the world of finance. Again, Seneca is fantastic at tracing requests. For every call, Seneca generates a unique identifier. This identifier can be traced across all the paths to where the call is going to, as follows:

```
var seneca = require("seneca")();

seneca.add({cmd: "greeter"}, function(args, callback){
  console.log(this.fixedargs['tx$']);
  callback(null, {message: "Hello " + args.name});
});
seneca.act({cmd: "greeter", name: "David"}, function(err, result) {
  console.log(this.fixedargs['tx$']);
});
```

Here, we are logging a dictionary that contains the transaction ID in Seneca to the terminal. So, if we execute it, we will get the following output:

```
2016-02-04T10:58:07.570Z zl0u7hj3hbeg/1454583487555/95159/- INFO hello
Seneca/1.0.0/zl0u7hj3hbeg/1454583487555/95159/-

3jlroj2n91da

3jlroj2n91da
```

You can see how all the requests in Seneca are traced: the framework assigns an ID and it gets propagated across endpoints. In this case, all our endpoints are in the local machine, but if we distribute them in different machines, the ID will still be the same.

With this unique ID, we will be able to reconstruct the journey of the customer data in our system, and ordering the requests with the associated timestamp, we can get an accurate picture of what the user was doing, how much time did every action take, what are the possible problems associated with delays, and so on. Usually, the logging combined with circuit breakers output information allows the engineers to solve issues within a very reduced time frame.

Auditing

Up till now, we have been using `console.log()` to output the data into the logs. This is a bad practice. It breaks the format of the logs and throws the content to the standard output.

Again, Seneca comes to the rescue:

```
var seneca = require("seneca")();

seneca.add({cmd: "greeter"}, function(args, callback){
  this.log.warn(this.fixedargs['tx$']);
  callback(null, {message: "Hello " + args.name});
});

seneca.act({cmd: "greeter", name: "David"}, function(err, result) {
  this.log.warn(this.fixedargs['tx$']);
});
```

Let's see what Seneca produces as output:

```
seneca   node index.js
2016-02-04T11:17:28.772Z wo10oa299tub/1454584648758/98550/- INFO hello
Seneca/1.0.0/wo10oa299tub/1454584648758/98550/-
2016-02-04T11:17:29.156Z wo10oa299tub/1454584648758/98550/- WARN - - ACT
02jlpyiux70s/9ca086d19x7n cmd:greeter 9ca086d19x7n
2016-02-04T11:17:29.157Z wo10oa299tub/1454584648758/98550/- WARN - - ACT
02jlpyiux70s/9ca086d19x7n cmd:greeter 9ca086d19x7n
```

As you can see, we are now outputting the transaction ID using the logger. We have produced a WARN message instead of a simple console dump. From now on, we can use Seneca log filters to hide the output of our actions in order to focus on what we are trying to find.

Seneca provides the following five levels of logging:

- **DEBUG**: This is used to debug applications when you are developing them and also trace problems in production systems.

- **INFO**: This log level is used to produce important messages about events such as a transaction has started or completed.

- **WARN**: This is the warning level. We use it when something bad happens in the system, but it is not critical, the user usually does not get affected; however, it is an indication that something is going in the wrong way.

- **ERROR**: This is used to log errors. Generally, the user gets affected by it and it also interrupts the flow.

- **FATAL**: This is the most catastrophic level. It is only used when a non-recoverable error has occurred and the system won't be able to function normally.

A way to produce logs in different levels is to use the associated functions. As we have seen earlier, we called `this.log.warn()` to log a warning. If we call the `this.log.fatal()` method, we will be logging a fatal error, and same with the other levels.

 Try to adjust the logs in your application as a part of the development process or you will regret the lack of information when something bad occurs in production.

In general, INFO, DEBUG, and WARN will be the most used log levels.

HTTP codes

HTTP codes are often ignored, but they are a really important mechanism to standardize responses from remote servers.

When a program (or user) issues a request to a server, there are a few things that could happen, as follows:

- It could be successful

- It could fail validation

- It could produce a server error

As you can see, the possibilities are endless. The problem that we now have is that HTTP was created for the communication between machines. How do we handle the fact that machines will be reading these codes?

HTTP solved this problem in a very elegant way: every single request has to be resolved with an HTTP code and these codes have ranges that indicate the nature of the code.

1xx – informational

The codes in the 100-199 range are purely informational. The most interesting code in this range is the 102 code. This code is used to specify that an operation is happening in the background and might take some time to complete.

2xx – success codes

Success codes are used to indicate a certain level of success in the HTTP request. It is the most common (and desired) codes.

The most common codes in this range are as follows:

- 200: Success: This code indicates a full success. Nothing went wrong even remotely.
- 201: Created: This code is used mainly for REST APIs when the client requests to create a new entity in the server.
- 203: Non-authoritative information: This code is intended to be used when, while routing the request through a transforming proxy, the origin responds with a 200.
- 204: No Content: This is a successful code, but there is no content coming back from the server. Sometimes, APIs returns 200, even if there is no content.
- 206: Partial Content: This code is used for paginated responses. A header is sent, specifying a range (and an offset) that the client will accept. If the response is bigger than the range, the server will reply with 206, indicating that there is more data to follow.

3xx – redirection

The codes in the 300 to 399 range indicate that the client must take some additional actions to complete the request.

The most common codes in this range are described as follows:

- 301: Moved permanently: This status code is indicating that the resource that the client was trying to get has been moved permanently to another location.

- `302: Found`: This code indicates that the user is required to perform a temporary redirect for some reason, but the browsers started implementing this code as `303 See Other`. This lead to the introduction of the 303 and `307 Temporary redirect` codes to disambiguate the overlap of behavior.

- `308 Permanent Redirect`: This code, as the name indicates, is used to specify a permanent redirect for a resource. It could be confused with 301, but there is a small difference, the 308 code does not allow the HTTP method to change.

4xx – client errors

The codes in the 400 to 499 range represent errors generated by the client. They indicate that there is a problem with the request. This range is particularly important as it is the way that HTTP servers have to indicate the clients that something is wrong with their request.

The common codes in this range are as follows:

- `400 Bad Request`: This code indicates that the request from the user is syntactically incorrect. There could be parameters missing or some of the values didn't pass validation.

- `401 Unauthorized`: This code represents a lack of authentication of the client. Usually, a valid login will fix this problem.

- `403 Forbidden`: This is similar to 401, but in this case, it is indicating that the user does not have enough privileges.

- `404 Not Found`: This means that the resource is not found in the server. This is the error that you get when you navigate to a page that does not exist.

5xx – server errors

This range indicates that there has been a processing error in the server. When a 5xx code is issued, it means that there was some sort of problem in the server and it cannot be fixed from the client.

Some of the codes in this range are as follows:

- `500 Internal Server Error`: This means that an error has occurred in the software in the server. There is no more information disclosed.

- `501 Not Implemented`: This error occurs when a client hits an endpoint that has not been implemented yet.

- `503 Service unavailable`: This code is issued when the server is not available for some reason, either an excess of the load or the server is down.

Why HTTP codes matter in microservices

The popular saying *don't reinvent the wheel* is one of my favorite principles when building software. HTTP codes are a standard, so everybody understands the consequences of the different codes.

When building microservices, you always need to keep in mind that your system will be interacting with proxies, caches, and other services that already speak HTTP so that they can react according to the response from the servers.

The best example of this is the circuit-breaker pattern. No matter how you implement it and what software you use, a circuit breaker has to understand that an HTTP request with 500 code is an error, so it can open the circuit accordingly.

In general, it is good practice to keep the codes of your application as accurate as possible as it will benefit your system in the long run.

Summary

In this chapter, you have learned how to build secure software (and not only microservices), although it is a subject big enough to write a full book on it. The problem with security is that companies usually see investing in security as burning money, but that is far from reality. I am a big fan of the 80-20 rule: 20% of time will give you 80% of features and the 20% of missing features will require 80% of the time.

In security, we really should be aiming for 100% coverage; however, the 80% shown in this chapter will cover majority of the cases. Anyway, as I mentioned before, a software engineer should be up to date with security as a flaw in the security of an application is the easiest way to kill a company.

We have also been talking about traceability and logging, one of the most ignored subjects in the modern software engineering that are becoming more and more important, especially if your software is built using a microservices approach.

6
Testing and Documenting Node.js Microservices

Until now, all that we have done is develop microservices and discuss the frameworks around the process of building software components. Now it is time to test all of them. Testing is the activity of validating the software that has been built. Validating is a very broad term. In this chapter, we are going to learn how to test microservices, not only from the functional point of view, but we will also learn how to test the performance of our applications, as well as other aspects such as integration with different modules. We will also build a proxy using Node.js to help us to inspect the inputs and outputs of our services so that we can validate that what we have designed is actually happening and, once again, reassure the versatility of a language, such as JavaScript, to quickly prototype features.

It is also nowadays a trend to release features with an A/B test, where we only enable the features for certain type of users, and then we collect metrics to see how the changes to our system are performing. In this chapter, we will build a microservice that is going to give us the capability of rolling out features in a controlled way.

On the other hand, we are going to document our application, which unfortunately, is a forgotten activity in traditional software development: I haven't found a single company where the documentation captures 100% the information needed by new developers.

We will cover the following topics in this chapter:

- **Functional testing**: In this section, we will learn how to test microservices and what a good testing strategy is. We will also get to study a tool called Postman to manually test our APIs, as well as build a proxy with Node.js to spy our connections.

- **Documenting microservices**: We will learn how to use Swagger to document our microservices using the open API standard. We will also generate the code from the YAML definition using an open source tool.

Functional testing

Testing is usually a time-consuming activity that does not get all the required attention while building a software.

Think about how a company evolves:

1. Someone comes up with an idea.
2. A few engineers/product people build the system.
3. The company goes to market.

There is no time to test more than the minimal required manual testing. Especially, when someone reads on the Internet that testing done right could take up to 40% of your development time, and once again, the common sense fails.

Automation is good and unit, integration, and end-to-end tests are a form of automation. By letting a computer test our software, we are drastically cutting down the human effort required to validate our software.

Think about how the software is developed. Even though our company likes to claim that *we are agile*, the truth is that every single software project has some level of iterative development, and testing is a part of every cycle, but generally, it is overlooked in favour of delivering new features.

By automating the majority (or a big chunk) of the testing, we are saving money, as shown in the following diagram:

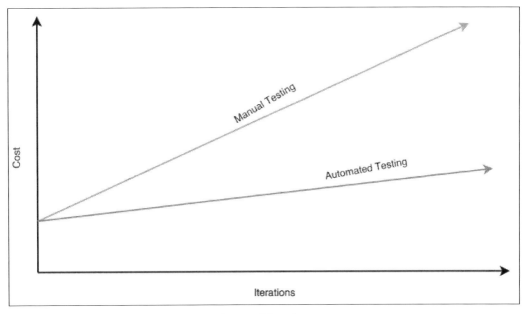

Costs and Iterations

Testing is actually a cost saver if is done right, and the key is doing it right, which is not always easy. How much testing is too much testing? Should we cover every single corner of our application? Do we really need deep performance testing?

These questions usually lead to a different stream of opinions, and the interesting thing is that there is not a single source of truth. It depends on the nature of your system.

In this chapter, we are going to learn a set of extensive testing techniques, which does not mean that we should be including all of them in our test plan, but at least we will be aware of the testing methodologies.

In the past seven years, Ruby on Rails has created a massive trend towards a new paradigm, called **Test-driven development** (**TDD**), up to a point that, nowadays, majority of the new development platforms are built with TDD in mind.

Personally, I am not a fierce adopter of TDD, but I like to take the good parts. Planning the test before the development helps to create modules with the right level of cohesion and define a clear and easy-to-test interface. In this chapter, we won't cover the TDD in depth, but we will mention it a few times and explain how to apply the exposed techniques to a TDD test plan.

The pyramid of automated testing

How to lay down your testing plan is a tricky question. No matter what you do, you will always end up with the sensation that *this is completely wrong*.

Before diving into the deep, let's define the different type of tests that we are going to be dealing with from the functional point of view, and what should they be designed for.

Unit tests

A **unit test** is a test that covers individual parts of the application without taking into account the integration with different modules. It is also called **white box testing** as the aim is to cover and verify as many branches as possible.

Generally, the way to measure the quality of our tests is the test coverage and it is measured in percentage. If our code spans over ten branches and our tests cover seven branches, our code coverage is 70%. This is a good indication of how reliable our test coverage is. However, it could be misleading as the tests could be flawed, or even though all the branches are tested, a different input would cause a different output that wasn't captured by a test.

In unit tests, as we don't interact with other modules, we will be making a heavy use of mocks and stubs in order to simulate responses from third-party systems and control the flow to hit the desired branch.

Integration tests

Integration tests, as the name suggests, are the tests designed to verify the integration of our module in the application environment. They are not designed to test the branches of our code, but business units, where we will be saving the data into databases, calling third-party web services or other microservices of our architecture.

These tests are the perfect tool for checking whether our service is behaving as expected, and sometimes, could be hard to maintain (more often than not).

During my years of experience, I haven't found a company where the integration testing is done right and there are a number of reasons for this, as stated in the following list:

- Some companies think that integration testing is expensive (and it is true) as it requires extra resources (such as databases and extra machines)

- Some other companies try to cover all the business cases just with unit testing, which depending on the business cases, could work, but it is far from ideal as unit tests make assumptions (mocks) that could give us a false confidence in our test suite

- Sometimes, integration tests are used to verify the code branches as if they were unit tests, which is time consuming as you need to work out the environment to make the integration test to hit the required branch

No matter how smart you want to be, integration testing is something that you want to do right, as it is the first real barrier in our software to prevent integration bugs from being released into production.

End-to-end tests

Here, we will demonstrate that our application actually works. In an integration test, we are invoking the services at code level. This means that we need to build the context of the service and then issue the call.

The difference with end-to-end testing is that, in end-to-end testing, we actually fully deploy our application and issue the required calls to execute the target code. However, many times, the engineers can decide to bundle both type of tests (integration and end-to-end tests) together, as the modern frameworks allow us to quickly run E2E tests as if they were integration tests.

As the integration tests, the target of the end-to-end tests is not to test all the paths of the application but test the use cases.

In end-to-end tests, we can find a few different modalities (paradigms) of testing, as follows:

- We can test our API issuing JSON requests (or other type of requests)

- We can test our UI using Selenium to emulate clicks on the DOM

- We can use a new paradigm called **behavior-driven development (BDD)** testing, where the use cases are mapped into actions in our application (clicks on the UI, requests in the API, and so on) and execute the use cases for which the application was built

End-to-end tests are usually very fragile and they get broken fairly easy. Depending on our application, we might get relaxed about these tests as the cost-value ratio is pretty low, but still, I would recommend having some of them covering at least the most basic and essential flows.

How much testing is too much?

Questions such as the following are not easy to answer, especially in fast paced businesses, like startups:

- Do we have too many integration tests?
- Should we aim for 100% unit test coverage?
- Why bother with Selenium tests if they break every second day for no reason?

There is always a compromise. Test coverage versus time consumed, and also, there is no simple and single answer to these questions.

The only useful guideline that I've found along the years is what the testing world calls the **pyramid of testing**, which is shown in the following figure. If you think for a moment, in the projects where you worked before, how many tests did you have in total? What percentage of these were integration tests and unit tests? What about end-to-end tests?:

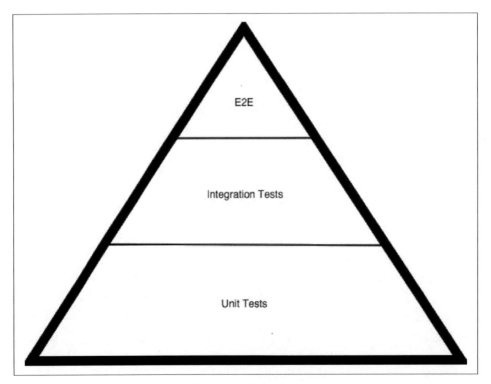

The pyramid of testing

The preceding pyramid shows the answers for these questions. In a healthy test plan, we should have a lot of unit tests: some integration tests and very few E2E tests.

The reason for this is very simple, majority of the problems can be caught within unit testing. Hitting the different branches of our code will verify the functionality of pretty much every functional case in our application, so it makes sense to have plenty of them in our test plan. Based on my experience, in a balanced test plan, around 70% of our tests should be unit tests. However, in a microservices-oriented architecture, especially with a dynamic language such as Node.js, this figure can easily go down and still be effective with our testing. The reasoning behind it is that Node.js allows you to write integration tests very quickly so that we can replace some unit tests by integration tests.

 Testing is a very well-documented, complex process. Trying to outsmart the existing methodologies could result in a hard-to-maintain and difficult-to-trust test suite.

Integration tests are responsible for catching integration problems, as shown in the following:

- Can our code call the SMS gateway?
- Would the connection to the database be OK?
- Are the HTTP headers being sent from our service?

Again, around 20% of our tests, based on my experience, should be integration tests; focus on the positive flows and some of the negative that depend on third-party modules.

When it comes down to E2E tests, they should be very limited and only test the main flows of the applications without going into too much detail. These details should be already captured by the unit and integration tests that are easy to fix in an event of failure. However, there is a catch here: when testing microservices in Node.js, 90% of the time, integration and E2E tests can be the same thing. Due to the dynamic nature of Node.js, we can test the rest API from the integration point of view (the full server running), but in reality, we will also be testing how our code behaves when integrated with other modules. We will see an example later in this chapter.

Testing microservices in Node.js

Node.js is an impressive language. The amount of libraries around any single aspect of the development is amazing. No matter how bizarre the task that you want to achieve in Node.js is, there will be always an npm module.

Regarding the testing, Node.js has a very powerful set of libraries, but two of them are especially popular: **Mocha** and **Chai**.

They are pretty much the industry standard for app testing and are very well maintained and upgraded.

Another interesting library is called **Sinon.JS**, and it is used for mocking, spying and stubbing methods. We will come back to these concepts in the following sections, but this library is basically used to simulate integrations with third parties without interacting with them.

Chai

This library is a BDD/TDD assertions library that can be used in conjunction with any other library to create high quality tests.

An assertion is a code statement that will either be fulfilled or throw an error, stopping the test and marking it as a failure:

```
5 should be equal to A
```

The preceding statement will be correct when the variable A contains the value 5. This is a very powerful tool to write easy-to-understand tests, and especially with Chai, we have access to assertions making use of the following three different interfaces:

* `should`
* `expect`
* `assert`

At the end of the day, every single condition can be checked using a single interface, but the fact that the library provides us with such a rich interface facilitates the verbosity of the tests in order to write clean, easy, and maintainable tests.

Let's install the library:

```
npm install chai
```

This will produce the following output:

```
├── assertion-error@1.0.1
├── type-detect@1.0.0
└── deep-eql@0.1.3 (type-detect@0.1.1)
```

This means that Chai depends on `assertion-error`, `type-detect`, and `deep-eql`. As you can see, this is a good indication that we will be able to check, with simple instructions, complex statements such as deep equality in objects or type matching.

Testing libraries such as Chai are not a direct dependency of our application, but a development dependency. We need them to develop applications, but they should not be shipped to production. This is a good reason to restructure our `package.json` and add Chai in the `devDependencies` dependency tag, as follows:

```
{
    "name": "chai-test",
    "version": "1.0.0",
    "description": "A test script",
    "main": "chai.js",
    "dependencies": {
    },
    "devDependencies": {
        "chai": "*"
    },
    "author": "David Gonzalez",
    "license": "ISC"
}
```

This will prevent our software to ship into production libraries such as Chai, which has nothing to do with the operation of our application.

Once we have installed Chai, we can start playing around with the interfaces.

BDD-style interfaces

Chai comes with two flavors of BDD interfaces. It is a matter of preference which one to use, but my personal recommendation is to use the one that makes you feel more comfortable in any situation.

Let's start with the `should` Interface. This one is a BDD-style interface, using something similar to the natural language, we can create assertions that will decide whether our test succeeds or fails:

```
myVar.should.be.a('string')
```

In order to be able to build sentences like the one before, we need to import the should module in our program:

```
var chai = require('chai');

chai.should();

var foo = "Hello world";
console.log(foo);

foo.should.equal('Hello world');
```

Although it looks like a bit of dark magic, it is really convenient when testing our code as we use something similar to the natural language to ensure that our code is meeting some criteria: *foo should be equal to 'Hello world'* has a direct translation to our test.

The second BDD-style interface provided by Chai is expect. Although it is very similar to should, it changes a bit of syntax in order to set expectations that the results have to meet.

Let's see the following example:

```
var expect = require('chai').expect;

var foo = "Hello world";

expect(foo).to.equal("Hello world");
```

As you can see, the style is very similar: a fluent interface that allows us to check whether the conditions for the test to succeed are met, but what happens if the conditions are not met?

Let's execute a simple Node.js program that fails in one of the conditions:

```
var expect = require('chai').expect;
var animals = ['cat', 'dog', 'parrot'];
expect(animals).to.have.length(4);
```

Now, let's execute the previous script, assuming that you have already installed Chai:

```
code/node_modules/chai/lib/chai/assertion.js:107
        throw new AssertionError(msg, {
            ^

AssertionError: expected [ 'cat', 'dog', 'parrot' ] to have a length of 4
but got 3
    at Object.<anonymous> (/Users/dgonzalez/Dropbox/Microservices with
Node/Writing Bundle/Chapter 6/code/chai.js:24:25)
    at Module._compile (module.js:460:26)
    at Object.Module._extensions..js (module.js:478:10)
    at Module.load (module.js:355:32)
    at Function.Module._load (module.js:310:12)
    at Function.Module.runMain (module.js:501:10)
    at startup (node.js:129:16)
    at node.js:814:3
```

An exception is thrown and the test fails. If all the conditions were validated, no exception would have been raised and the test would have succeeded.

As you can see, there are a number of natural language words that we can use for our tests using both `expect` and `should` interfaces. The full list can be found in the Chai documentation (`http://chaijs.com/api/bdd/#-include-value-`), but let's explain some of the most interesting ones in the following list:

- `not`: This word is used to negate the assertions following in the chain. For example, `expect("some string").to.not.equal("Other String")` will pass.

- `deep`: This word is one of the most interesting of all the collection. It is used to deep-compare objects, which is the quickest way to carry on a full equal comparison. For example, `expect(foo).to.deep.equal({name: "David"})` will succeed if `foo` is a JavaScript object with one property called `name` with the `"David"` string value.

- `any/all`: This is used to check whether the dictionary or object contains any of the keys in the given list so that `expect(foo).to.have.any.keys("name", "surname")` will succeed if `foo` contains any of the given keys, and `expect(foo).to.have.all.keys("name", "surname")` will only succeed if it has all of the keys.

- ok: This is an interesting one. As you probably know, JavaScript has a few pitfalls, and one of them is the true/false evaluation of expressions. With ok, we can abstract all the mess and do something similar to the following list of expressions:
    - ○ expect('everything').to.be.ok: 'everything' is a string and it will be evaluated to ok
    - ○ expect(undefined).to.not.be.ok: Undefined is not ok in the JavaScript world, so this assertion will succeed

- above: This is a very useful word to check whether an array or collection contains a number of elements above a certain threshold, as follows: expect([1,2,3]).to.have.length.above(2)

As you can see, the Chai API for fluent assertions is quite rich and enables us to write very descriptive tests that are easy to maintain.

Now, you may be asking yourself, why have two flavors of the same interface that pretty much work the same? Well, they functionally do the same, however, take a look at the detail:

- expect provides a starting point in your chainable language
- should extends the Object.prototype signature to add the chainable language to every single object in JavaScript

From Node.js' point of view, both of them are fine, although the fact that should is instrumenting the prototype of Object could be a reason to be a bit paranoid about using it as it is intrusive.

Assertions interface

The **assertions** interface matches the most common old-fashioned tests assertion library. In this flavor, we need to be specific about what we want to test, and there is no such thing as fluent chaining of expressions:

```
var assert = require('chai').assert;
var myStringVar = 'Here is my string';
// No message:
assert.typeOf(myStringVar, 'string');
// With message:
assert.typeOf(myStringVar, 'string', 'myStringVar is not string
  type.');
// Asserting on length:
assert.lengthOf(myStringVar, 17);
```

There is really nothing more to go in depth if you have already used any of the existing test libraries in any language.

Mocha

Mocha is, in my opinion, one of the most convenient testing frameworks that I have ever used in my professional life. It follows the principles of **behavior-driven development testing (BDDT)**, where the test describes a use case of the application and uses the assertions from another library to verify the outcome of the executed code.

Although it sounds a bit complicated, it is really convenient to ensure that our code is covered from the functional and technical point of view, as we will be mirroring the requirements used to build the application into automated tests that verifies them.

Let's start with a simple example. Mocha is a bit different from any other library, as it defines its own **domain-specific language (DSL)** that needs to be executed with Mocha instead of Node.js. It is an extension of the language.

First we need to install Mocha in the system:

```
npm install mocha -g
```

This will produce an output similar to the following image:

```
/usr/local/bin/mocha -> /usr/local/lib/node_modules/mocha/bin/mocha
/usr/local/bin/_mocha -> /usr/local/lib/node_modules/mocha/bin/_mocha
mocha@2.4.5 /usr/local/lib/node_modules/mocha
├── escape-string-regexp@1.0.2
├── supports-color@1.2.0
├── growl@1.8.1
├── diff@1.4.0
├── commander@2.3.0
├── jade@0.26.3 (commander@0.6.1, mkdirp@0.3.0)
├── debug@2.2.0 (ms@0.7.1)
├── mkdirp@0.5.1 (minimist@0.0.8)
└── glob@3.2.3 (graceful-fs@2.0.3, inherits@2.0.1, minimatch@0.2.14)
```

From now on, we have a new command in our system: mocha.

The next step is to write a test using Mocha:

```
function rollDice() {
  return Math.floor(Math.random() * 6) + 1;
}

require('chai').should();
var expect = require('chai').expect;

describe('When a customer rolls a dice', function(){

  it('should return an integer number', function() {
    expect(rollDice()).to.be.an('number');
  });

  it('should get a number below 7', function(){
    rollDice().should.be.below(7);
  });

  it('should get a number bigger than 0', function(){
    rollDice().should.be.above(0);
  });

  it('should not be null', function() {
    expect(rollDice()).to.not.be.null;
  });

  it('should not be undefined', function() {
    expect(rollDice()).to.not.be.undefined;
  });
});
```

The preceding example is simple. A function that rolls a dice and returns an integer number from 1 to 6. Now we need to think a bit about the use cases and the requirements:

- The number has to be an integer
- This integer has to be below 7
- It has to be above 0, dice don't have negative numbers
- The function cannot return `null`
- The function cannot return `undefined`

This covers pretty much every corner case about rolling a dice in Node.js. What we are doing is describing situations that we certainly want to test, in order to safely make changes to the software without breaking the existing functionality.

These five use cases are an exact map to the tests written earlier:

- **We describe the situation**: *When a customer rolls a dice*
- **Conditions get verified**: *It should return an integer number*

Let's run the previous test and check the results:

```
mocha tests.js
```

This should return something similar to the following screenshot:

As you can see, Mocha returns a comprehensive report on what is going on in the tests. In this case, all of them pass, so we don't need to be worried about problems.

Let's force some of the tests to fail:

```
function rollDice() {
  return -1 * Math.floor(Math.random() * 6) + 1;
}

require('chai').should();
var expect = require('chai').expect;

describe('When a customer rolls a dice', function(){

  it('should return an integer number', function() {
    expect(rollDice()).to.be.an('number');
  });

  it('should get a number below 7', function(){
```

```
      rollDice().should.be.below(7);
  });

  it('should get a number bigger than 0', function(){
      rollDice().should.be.above(0);
  });

  it('should not be null', function() {
      expect(rollDice()).to.not.be.null;
  });

  it('should not be undefined', function() {
      expect(rollDice()).to.not.be.undefined;
  });
});
```

Accidentally, someone has bumped a code fragment into the `rollDice()` function, which makes the function return a number that does not meet some of the requirements. Let's run Mocha again, as shown in the following image:

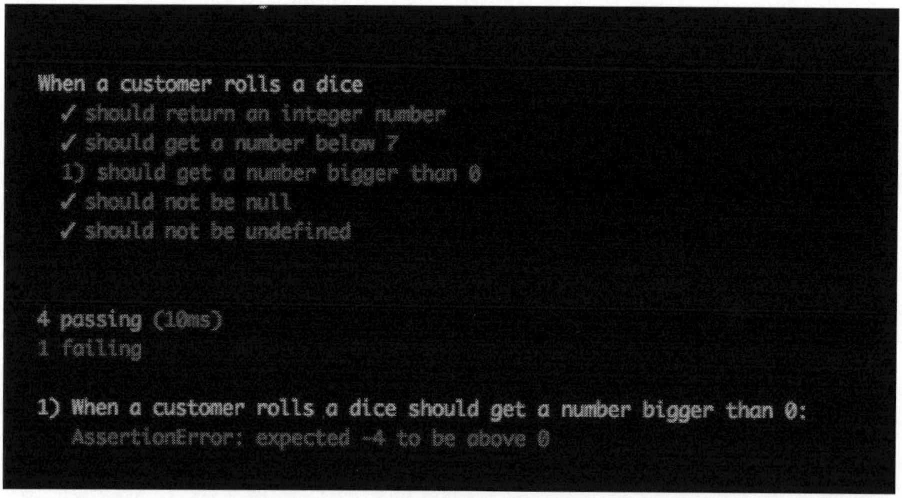

Now, we can see the report returning one error: the method is returning -4, where it should always return a number bigger than 0.

Also, one of the benefits of this type of testing in Node.js using Mocha and Chai is the time. Tests run very fast so that it is easy to receive feedback if we have broken something. The preceding suite ran in 10ms.

Sinon.JS – a mocking framework

The previous two chapters have been focused on asserting conditions on return values of functions, but what happens when our function does not return any value? The only correct measurement is to check whether the method was called or not. Also, what if one of our modules is calling a third-party web service, but we don't want our tests to call the remote server?

For answering these questions, we have two conceptual tools called mocks and spies, and Node.js has the perfect library to implement them: Sinon.JS.

First install it, as follows:

```
npm install sinon
```

The preceding command should produce the following output:

Now let's explain how it works through an example:

```
function calculateHypotenuse(x, y, callback) {
    callback(null, Math.sqrt(x*x + y*x));
}

calculateHypotenuse(3, 3, function(err, result){
    console.log(result);
});
```

This simple script calculates the hypotenuse of a triangle, given the length of the other two sides of the triangle. One of the tests that we want to carry on is the fact that the callback is executed with the right list of arguments supplied. What we need to accomplish such task is what Sinon.JS calls a spy:

```
var sinon = require('sinon');

require('chai').should();

function calculateHypotenuse(x, y, callback) {
    callback(null, Math.sqrt(x*x + y*x));
}

describe("When the user calculates the hypotenuse", function(){
```

```
it("should execute the callback passed as argument", function() {
  var callback = sinon.spy();
  calculateHypotenuse(3, 3, callback);
  callback.called.should.be.true;
});
});
```

Once again, we are using Mocha to run the script and Chai to verify the results in the test through the `should` interface, as shown in the following image:

The important line in the preceding script is:

```
var callback = sinon.spy();
```

Here, we are creating the spy and injecting it into the function as a callback. This function created by Sinon.JS is actually not only a function, but a full object with a few interesting points of information. Sinon.JS does that, taking advantage of the dynamic nature of JavaScript. You can actually see what is in this object by dumping it into the console with `console.log()`.

Another very powerful tool in Sinon.JS are the stubs. **Stubs** are very similar to mocks (identical at practical effects in JavaScript) and allow us to fake functions to simulate the required return:

```
var sinon = require('sinon');
var expect = require('chai').expect;

function rollDice() {
  return -1 * Math.floor(Math.random() * 6) + 1;
}
describe("When rollDice gets called", function() {
  it("Math#random should be called with no arguments", function() {
    sinon.stub(Math, "random");
    rollDice();
    console.log(Math.random.calledWith());
  });
})
```

In this case, we have stubbed the `Math#random` method, which causes the method to be some sort of overloaded empty function (it does not issue the get call) that records stats on what or how it was called.

There is one catch in the preceding code: we never restored the `random()` method back and this is quite dangerous. It has a massive side effect, as other tests will see the `Math#random` method as a stub, not as the original one, and it can lead to us coding our tests according to invalid information.

In order to prevent this, we need to make use of the `before()` and `after()` methods from Mocha:

```
var sinon = require('sinon');
var expect = require('chai').expect;

var sinon = require('sinon');
var expect = require('chai').expect;

function rollDice() {
   return -1 * Math.floor(Math.random() * 6) + 1;
}
describe("When rollDice gets called", function() {

   it("Math#random should be called with no arguments", function() {
      sinon.stub(Math, "random");
      rollDice();
      console.log(Math.random.calledWith());
   });
after(function(){
   Math.random.restore();
   });
});
```

If you pay attention to the highlighted code, we are telling Sinon.JS to restore the original method that was stubbed inside one of the `it` blocks, so that if another `describe` block makes use of `http.get`, we won't see the stub, but the original method.

The `before()` and `after()` methods are very helpful to set up and wind down the context for the tests. However, you need to be careful with the scope where they are executed as it could lead to test interactions.

Mocha has a few flavors of before and after:

- `before(callback)`: This is executed before the current scope (at the beginning of the `describe` block in the preceding code)
- `after(callback)`: This is executed after the current scope (at the end of the `describe` block in the preceding code)
- `beforeEach(callback)`: This is executed at the beginning of every element in the current scope (before each `it` in the preceding example)
- `afterEach(callback)`: This is executed at the end of every element in the current scope (after every `it` in the preceding example)

Another interesting feature in Sinon.JS is the time manipulation. Some of the tests need to execute periodic tasks or respond after a certain time of an event's occurrence. With Sinon.JS, we can dictate time as one of the parameters of our tests:

```
var sinon = require('sinon');
var expect = require('chai').expect

function areWeThereYet(callback) {

  setTimeout(function() {
    callback.apply(this);
  }, 10);

}

var clock;

before(function(){
  clock = sinon.useFakeTimers();
});

it("callback gets called after 10ms", function () {
  var callback = sinon.spy();
  var throttled = areWeThereYet(callback);

  areWeThereYet(callback);

  clock.tick(9);
  expect(callback.notCalled).to.be.true;

  clock.tick(1);
```

```
    expect(callback.notCalled).to.be.false;
});

after(function(){
  clock.restore();
});
```

As you can see, we can now control the time in our tests.

Testing a real microservice

Now, it is time to test a real microservice in order to get a general picture of the full test suite.

Our microservice is going to use Express, and it will filter an input text to remove what the search engines call **stop words**: *words with less than three characters and words that are banned.*

Let's see the code:

```
var _ = require('lodash');
var express = require('express');

var bannedWords = ["kitten", "puppy", "parrot"];

function removeStopWords (text, callback) {
  var words = text.split(' ');
  var validWords = [];
  _(words).forEach(function(word, index) {
    var addWord = true;

    if (word.length < 3) {
      addWord = false;
    }

    if(addWord && bannedWords.indexOf(word) > -1) {
      addWord = false;
    }

    if (addWord) {
      validWords.push(word);
    }

    // Last iteration:
    if (index == (words.length - 1)) {
```

```
        callback(null, validWords.join(" "));
    }
  });
}
var app = express();

app.get('/filter', function(req, res) {
  removeStopWords(req.query.text, function(err, response){
    res.send(response);
  });
});

app.listen(3000, function() {
  console.log("app started in port 3000");
});
```

As you can see, the service is pretty small, so it is the perfect example for explaining how to write unit, integration, and E2E tests. In this case, as we stated before, E2E and integration tests are going to be the exact same as testing the service through the REST API will be equivalent to testing the system from the end-to-end point of view, but also how our component is integrated within the system. Given that, if we were to add a UI, we would have to split integration tests from E2E in order to ensure the quality.

TDD – Test-driven development

Our service is done and working. However, now we want to unit test it, but we find some problems:

- The function that we want to unit test is not visible outside the main `.js` file
- The server code is tightly coupled to the functional code and has bad cohesion

Here TDD comes to the rescue; we should always ask ourselves "how am I going to test this function when writing software?" It does not mean that we should modify our software with the specific purpose of testing, but if you are having problems while testing a part of your program, more than likely, you should look into cohesion and coupling, as it is a good indication of problems. Let's take a look at the following file:

```
var _ = require('lodash');
var express = require('express');

module.exports = function(options) {
```

```
      bannedWords = [];
      if (typeof options !== 'undefined') {
        console.log(options);
        bannedWords = options.bannedWords || [];
      }

      return function bannedWords(text, callback) {
        var words = text.split(' ');
        var validWords = [];
        _(words).forEach(function(word, index) {
          var addWord = true;

          if (word.length < 3) {
            addWord = false;
          }

          if(addWord && bannedWords.indexOf(word) > -1) {
            addWord = false;
          }

          if (addWord) {
            validWords.push(word);
          }

          // Last iteration:
          if (index == (words.length - 1)) {
            callback(null, validWords.join(" "));
          }
        });
      }
    }
```

This file is a module that, in my opinion, is highly reusable and has good cohesion:

- We can import it everywhere (even in a browser)
- The banned words can be injected when creating the module (very useful for testing)
- It is not tangled with the application code

Laying down the code this way, our application module will look similar to the following:

```
var _ = require('lodash');
var express = require('express');

var removeStopWords = require('./remove-stop-words')({bannedWords:
    ["kitten", "puppy", "parrot"]});

var app = express();

app.get('filter', function(req, res) {
    res.send(removeStopWords(req.query.text));
});

app.listen(3000, function() {
    console.log("app started in port 3000");
});
```

As you can see, we have clearly separated the business unit (the function that captures the business logic) from the operational unit (the setup of the server).

As I mentioned before, I am not a big fan of writing the tests prior to the code, but they should be written (in my opinion) alongside the code, but always having in mind the question mentioned before.

There seem to be a push in companies to adopt a TDD methodology, but it could lead to a significant inefficiency, especially if the business requirements are unclear (as they are 90% of the time) and we face changes along the development process.

Unit testing

Now that our code is in a better shape, we are going to unit test our function. We will use Mocha and Chai to accomplish such task:

```
var removeStopWords = require('./remove-stop-words')({bannedWords:
    ["kitten", "parrot"]});

var chai = require('chai');
var assert = chai.assert;
chai.should();
var expect = chai.expect;

describe('When executing "removeStopWords"', function() {

    it('should remove words with less than 3 chars of length',
        function() {
```

```
  removeStopWords('my small list of words', function(err,
    response) {
    expect(response).to.equal("small list words");
  });
});

it('should remove extra white spaces', function() {
  removeStopWords('my small       list of words', function(err,
    response) {
    expect(response).to.equal("small list words");
  });
});

it('should remove banned words', function() {
  removeStopWords('My kitten is sleeping', function(err,
    response) {
    expect(response).to.equal("sleeping");
  });
});

it('should not fail with null as input', function() {
  removeStopWords(null, function(err, response) {
    expect(response).to.equal("small list words");
  });
});

it('should fail if the input is not a string', function() {
  try {
    removeStopWords(5, function(err, response) {});
    assert.fail();
  }
  catch(err) {
  }
});
});
```

As you can see, we have covered pretty much every single case and branch inside our application, but how is our code coverage looking?

Until now, we have mentioned it, but never actually measured it. We are going to use one tool, called **Istanbul**, to measure the test coverage:

```
npm install -g istanbul
```

This should install Istanbul. Now we need to run the coverage report:

```
istanbul cover _mocha my-tests.js
```

This will produce an output similar to the one shown in the following image:

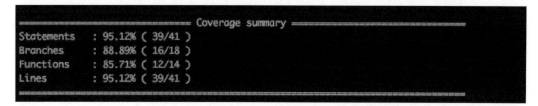

This will also generate a coverage report in HTML, pointing out which lines, functions, branches, and statements are not being covered, as shown in the following screenshot:

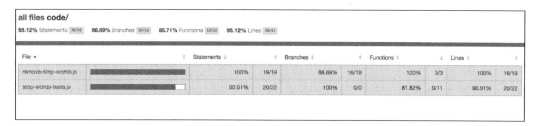

As you can see, we are looking pretty well. Our code (not the tests) is actually well covered, especially if we look into the detailed report for our code file, as shown in the following image:

```
all files / code/ remove-stop-words.js

100% Statements 19/19    88.89% Branches 16/18    100% Functions 3/3    100% Lines 19/19


 1   1×   var _ = require('lodash');
 2   1×   var express = require('express');
 3
 4   1×   module.exports = function(options) {
 5   1×       var bannedWords = [];
 6   1×     E if (typeof options !== 'undefined') {
 7   1×           bannedWords = options.bannedWords || [];
 8           }
 9
10   1×       return function removeBannedWords(text, callback) {
11   5×           var words = text != null && typeof text !== 'undefined' ? text.split(' ') : [];
12   4×           var validWords = [];
13   4×           _(words).forEach(function(word, index) {
14  20×               var addWord = true;
15
16  20×               if (word.length < 3) {
17  12×                   addWord = false;
18                   }
19  20×               if(addWord && bannedWords.indexOf(word) > -1) {
20   1×                   addWord = false;
21                   }
22
23  20×               if (addWord) {
24   7×                   validWords.push(word);
25                   }
26
27                   // Last iteration:
28  20×               if (index == (words.length - 1)) {
29   3×                   callback(null, validWords.join(" "));
30                   }
31               });
32           }
33       }
34
```

We can see that only one branch (the `or` operator in line **7**) is not covered and the `if` operator in line **6** never diverted to the `else` operator.

We also got information about the number of times a line is executed: it is showing in the vertical bar beside the line number. This information is also very useful to spot the hot areas of our application where an optimization will benefit the most.

Regarding the right level of coverage, in this example, it is fairly easy to go up to 90%+, but unfortunately, it is not that easy in production systems:

- Code is a lot more complex
- Time is always a constraint
- Testing might not be seen as productive time

However, you should exercise caution when working with a dynamic language. In Java or C#, calling a function that does not exist results in a compilation time error; whereas in JavaScript, it will result in a runtime error. The only real barrier is the testing (manual or automated), so it is a good practice to ensure that at least every line is executed once. In general code coverage, over 75% should be good enough for the majority of cases.

End-to-end testing

In order to test our application end to end, we are going to need a server running it. Usually, end-to-end tests are executed against a controlled environment, such as a QA box or a pre-production machine, to verify that our about-to-be-deployed software is behaving as expected.

In this case, our application is an API, so we are going to create the end-to-end tests, which at the same time, are going to be used as integration tests.

However, in a full application, we might want to have a clear separation between the integration and end-to-end tests and use something like Selenium to test our application from the UI point of view.

Selenium is a framework that allows our code to send instructions to the browser, as follows:

- Click the button with the `button1` ID
- Hover over the `div` element with the CSS class `highlighted`

In this way, we can ensure that our app flows work as expected, end to end, and our next release is not going to break the key flows of our app.

Let's focus on the end-to-end tests for our microservice. We have been using Chai and Mocha with their corresponding assertion interfaces to unit test our software, and Sinon.JS to mock services functions and other elements to avoid the calls being propagated to third-party web services or get a controlled response from one method.

Now, in our end-to-end test plan, we actually want to issue the calls to our service and get the response to validate the results.

The first thing we need to do is run our microservice somewhere. We are going to use our local machine just for convenience, but we can execute these tests in a continuous development environment against a QA machine.

So, let's start the server:

```
node stop-words.js
```

I call my script `stop-words.js` for convenience. Once the server is running, we are ready to start testing. In some situations, we might want our test to start and stop the server so that everything is self-contained. Let's see a small example about how to do it:

```
var express = require('express');

var myServer = express();

var chai = require('chai');

myServer.get('/endpoint', function(req, res){
  res.send('endpoint reached');
});

var serverHandler;

before(function(){
  serverHandler - myServer.listen(3000);
});

describe("When executing 'GET' into /endpoint", function(){
  it("should return 'endpoint reached'", function(){
    // Your test logic here. http://localhost:3000 is your server.
  });
});

after(function(){
  serverHandler.close();
});
```

As you can see, Express provides a handler to operate the server programmatically, so it is as simple as making use of the `before()` and `after()` functions to do the trick.

In our example, we are going to assume that the server is running. In order to issue the requests, we are going to use a library called `request` to issue the calls to the server.

The way to install it, as usual, is to execute `npm install request`. Once it is finished, we can make use of this amazing library:

```
var chai = require('chai');
var chaiHttp = require('chai-http');
var expect = chai.expect;
chai.use(chaiHttp);

describe("when we issue a 'GET' to /filter with text='aaaa bbbb
  cccc'", function(){
  it("should return HTTP 200", function(done) {
    chai.request('http://localhost:3000')
      .get('/filter')
      .query({text: 'aa bb ccccc'}).end(function(req, res){
        expect(res.status).to.equal(200);
        done();
      });
  });
});

describe("when we issue a 'GET' to /filter with text='aa bb
  ccccc'", function(){
  it("should return 'ccccc'", function(done) {
    chai.request('http://localhost:3000')
      .get('/filter')
      .query({text: 'aa bb ccccc'}).end(function(req, res){
        expect(res.text).to.equal('ccccc');
        done();
      });
  });
});

describe("when we issue a 'GET' to /filter with text='aa bb cc'",
  function(){
  it("should return ''", function(done) {
    chai.request('http://localhost:3000')
      .get('/filter')
      .query({text: 'aa bb cc'}).end(function(req, res){
```

```
            expect(res.text).to.equal('');
            done();
        });
    });
});
```

With the simple test from earlier, we managed to test our server in a way that ensures that every single mobile part of the application has been executed.

There is a particularity here that we didn't have before:

```
it("should return 'ccccc'", function(done) {
    chai.request('http://localhost:3000')
      .get('/filter')
      .query({text: 'aa bb ccccc'}).end(function(req, res){
        expect(res.text).to.equal('ccccc');
        done();
      });
});
```

If you take a look at the highlighted code, you can see a new callback called done. This callback has one mission: prevent the test from finishing until it is called, so that the HTTP request has time to be executed and return the appropriated value. Remember, Node.js is asynchronous, there is no such thing as a thread being blocked until one operation finishes.

Other than that, we are using a new DSL introduced by chai-http to build get requests.

This language allows us to build a large range of combinations, consider the following, for example:

```
chai.request('http://mydomain.com')
  .post('/myform')
  .field('_method', 'put')
  .field('username', 'dgonzalez')
  .field('password', '123456').end(...)
```

In the preceding request, we are submitting a form that looks like a login, so that in the end() function, we can assert the return from the server.

There are an endless number of combinations to test our APIs with chai-http.

Manual testing – the necessary evil

No matter how much effort we put in to our automated testing, there will always be a number of manual tests executed.

Sometimes, we need to do it just when we are developing our API, as we want to see the messages going from our client to the server, but some other times, we just want to hit our endpoints with a pre-forged request to cause the software to execute as we expect.

In the first case, we are going to take the advantage of Node.js and its dynamic nature to build a proxy that will sniff all the requests and log them to a terminal so that we can debug what is going on. This technique can be used to leverage the communication between two microservices and see what is going on without interrupting the flow.

In the second case, we are going to use software called Postman to issue requests against our server in a controlled way.

Building a proxy to debug our microservices

My first contact with Node.js was exactly due to this problem: two servers sending messages to each other, causing misbehavior without an apparent cause.

It is a very common problem that has many already-working solutions (man-in-the-middle proxies basically), but we are going to demonstrate how powerful Node.js is:

```
var http = require('http');
var httpProxy = require('http-proxy');
var proxy = httpProxy.createProxyServer({});

http.createServer(function(req, res) {
  console.log(req.rawHeaders);
  proxy.web(req, res, { target: 'http://localhost:3000' });
}).listen(4000);
```

If you remember from the previous section, our `stop-words.js` program was running on the port `3000`. What we have done with this code is create a proxy using `http-proxy`, that tunnels all the requests made on the port `4000` into the port `3000` after logging the headers into the console.

If we run the program after installing all the dependencies with the `npm install` command in the root of the project, we can see how effectively the proxy is logging the requests and tunneling them into the target host:

```
curl http://localhost:4000/filter?text=aaa
```

This will produce the following output:

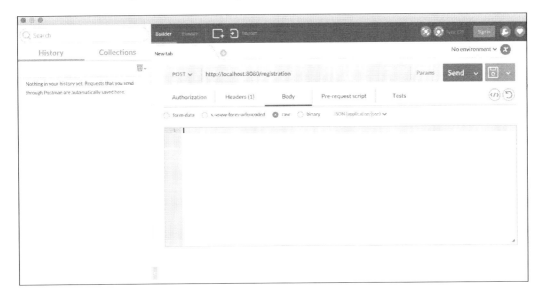

```
⇒ code  node proxy.js
[ 'Host',
  'localhost:4000',
  'User-Agent',
  'curl/7.43.0',
  'Accept',
  '*/*' ]
```

This example is very simplistic, but this small proxy could virtually be deployed anywhere in between our microservices and give us very valuable information about what is going on in the network.

Postman

Out of all the software that we can find on the Internet for testing APIs, Postman is my favorite. It started as a extension for Google Chrome, but nowadays, has taken the form of a standalone app built on the Chrome runtime.

It can be found in the Chrome web store, and it is free (so you don't need to pay for it), although it has a version for teams with more advanced features that is paid.

The interface is very concise and simple, as shown in the following screenshot:

On the left-hand side, we can see the **History** of requests, as well as the **Collections** of requests, which will be very handy for when we are working on a long-term project and we have some complicated requests to be built.

We are going to use again our `stop-words.js` microservice to show how powerful Postman can be.

Therefore, the first thing is to make sure that our microservice is running. Once it is, let's issue a request from Postman, as shown in the following screenshot:

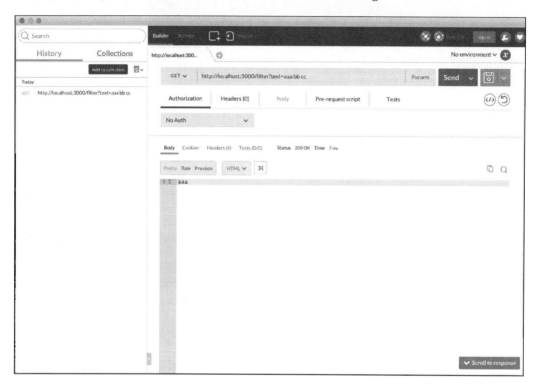

As simple as that, we have issued the request for our service (using the **GET** verb) and it has replied with the text filtered: very simple and effective.

Now imagine that we want to execute that call over Node.js. Postman comes with a very interesting feature, which is generating the code for the requests that we issue from the interface. If you click on the icon under the save button on the right-hand side of the window, the appearing screen will do the magic:

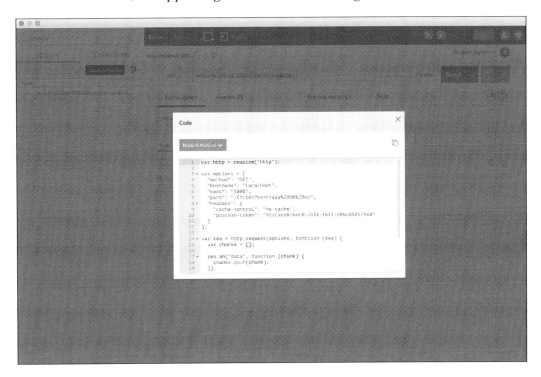

Let's take a look at the generated code:

```
var http = require("http");

var options = {
  "method": "GET",
  "hostname": "localhost",
  "port": "3000",
  "path": "/filter?text=aaa%20bb%20cc",
  "headers": {
    "cache-control": "no-cache",
    "postman-token": "912cacd8-bcc0-213f-f6ff-f0bcd98579c0"
  }
};

var req = http.request(options, function (res) {
```

```
var chunks = [];

res.on("data", function (chunk) {
  chunks.push(chunk);
});

res.on("end", function () {
  var body = Buffer.concat(chunks);
  console.log(body.toString());
});
});

req.end();
```

It is quite an easy code to understand, especially if you are familiar with the HTTP library.

With Postman, we can also send cookies, headers, and forms to the servers in order to mimic the authentication that an application will fulfill by sending the authentication token or cookie across.

Let's redirect our request to the proxy that we created in the preceding section, as shown in the following screenshot:

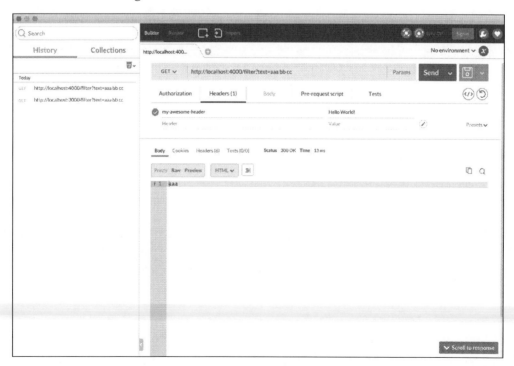

If you have the proxy and the `stop-words.js` microservice running, you should see something similar to the following output in the proxy:

```
⇒ code node proxy.js
[ 'Host',
  'localhost:4000',
  'User-Agent',
  'curl/7.43.0',
  'Accept',
  '*/*' ]
[ 'Host',
  'localhost:4000',
  'Connection',
  'keep-alive',
  'Cache-Control',
  'no-cache',
  'my-awesome-header',
  'Hello World!',
  'User-Agent',
  'Mozilla/5.0 (Macintosh; Intel Mac OS X 10_11_0) AppleWebKit/537.36 (KHTML, like Gecko) Chrome/48.0.2564.116 Safari/537.36',
  'Postman-Token',
  '9381e356-2d24-8ffe-82c6-6b16c837af18',
  'Accept',
  '*/*',
  'Accept-Encoding',
  'gzip, deflate, sdch',
  'Accept-Language',
  'es-ES,es;q=0.8,en;q=0.6' ]
```

The header that we sent over with Postman, **my-awesome-header**, will show up in the list of raw headers.

Documenting microservices

In this section, we are going to learn how to use Swagger to document APIs. Swagger is an API manager that follows the **Open API standard**, so that it is a *common language* for all the API creators. We will discuss how to write definitions and why it is so important to agree on how to describe resources.

Documenting APIs with Swagger

Documentation is always a problem. No matter how hard you try, it will always eventually go out of date. Luckily, in the past few years, there has been a push into producing a high quality documentation for REST APIs.

API managers have played a key role in it, and Swagger is particularly an interesting platform to look at. More than a module for documentation, Swagger manages your API in a such way that gives you a holistic view of your work.

Let's start installing it:

```
npm install -g swagger
```

This will install Swagger system-wide, so it will be another command in our system. Now, we need to create a project using it:

```
swagger project create my-project
```

This command will allow you to choose different web frameworks. We are going to choose Express, as it is the one that we have already been using. The output of the preceding command is shown in the following screenshot:

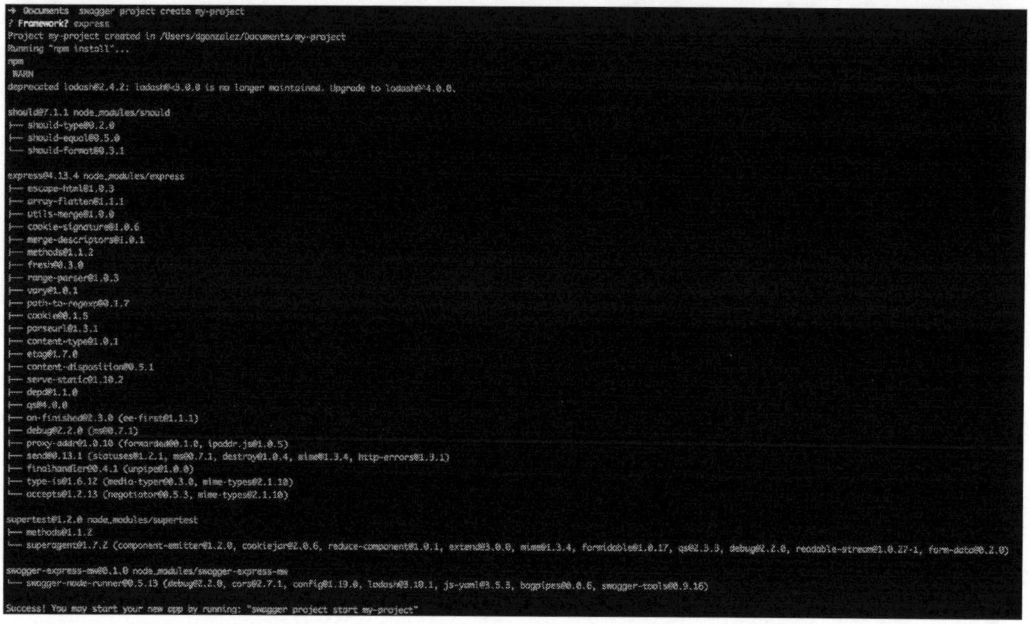

This screenshot is showing how to start a project with Swagger

Now we can find a new folder, called `my-project`, that looks like the following image:

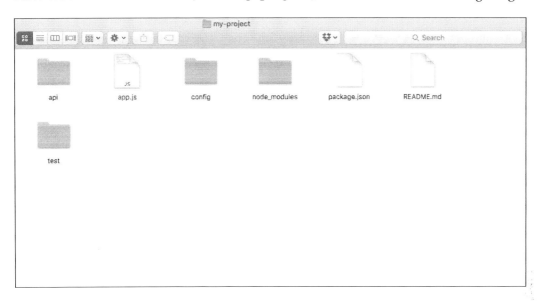

The structure is self-explanatory and it is the common layout of a Node.js application:

- `api`: Here, our API code will lay down
- `config`: All the configuration sits in here
- `node_modules`: This is a folder with all the dependencies required to run our application
- `test`: This is where Swagger has generated some dummy tests and where we could add our own tests

Swagger comes with an impressive feature: an embedded editor that allows you to model the endpoints of your API. In order to run it, from within the generated folder, execute the following command:

```
Swagger project edit
```

It will open Swagger Editor in the default browser, with a window similar to the following image:

Swagger makes use of **Yet Another Markup Language** (**YAML**). It is a language that is very similar to **JSON**, but with a different syntax.

In this document, we can customize a number of things, such as paths (routes in our application). Let's take a look at the path generated by Swagger:

```
/hello:
  # binds a127 app logic to a route
  x-swagger-router-controller: hello_world
  get:
    description: Returns 'Hello' to the caller
    # used as the method name of the controller
    operationId: hello
    parameters:
      - name: name
```

```
        in: query
        description: The name of the person to whom to say hello
        required: false
        type: string
    responses:
      "200":
        description: Success
        schema:
          # a pointer to a definition
          $ref: "#/definitions/HelloWorldResponse"
      # responses may fall through to errors
      default:
        description: Error
        schema:
          $ref: "#/definitions/ErrorResponse"
```

The definition is self-documented. Basically, we will configure the parameters used by our endpoint, but in a declarative way. This endpoint is mapping the incoming actions into the `hello_world` controller, and specifically into the `hello` method, which is defined by the `id` operation. Let's see what Swagger has generated for us in this controller:

```
'use strict';

var util = require('util');

module.exports = {
  hello: hello
};

function hello(req, res) {
  var name = req.swagger.params.name.value || 'stranger';
  var hello = util.format('Hello, %s!', name);
  res.json(hello);
}
```

This code can be found in the `api/controllers` folder of the project. As you can see, it is a pretty standard Express controller packed as a module (well-cohesioned). The only strange line is the first one in the `hello` function, where we pick up the parameters from Swagger. We will come back to this later, once we run the project.

The second part of the endpoint is the responses. As we can see, we are referencing two definitions: `HelloWorldResponse` for `http code 200` and `ErrorResponse` for the rest of the codes. These objects are defined in the following code:

```
definitions:
  HelloWorldResponse:
    required:
      - message
    properties:
      message:
        type: string
  ErrorResponse:
    required:
      - message
    properties:
      message:
        type: string
```

This is something really interesting, although we are using a dynamic language, the contract is being defined by Swagger so that we have a language-agnostic definition that can be consumed by a number of different technologies, respecting the principle of technology heterogeneity that we were talking about earlier in *Chapter 1, Microservices Architecture*, and *Chapter 2, Microservices in Node.js – Seneca and PM2 Alternatives*.

After explaining how the definition works, it is time to start the server:

```
swagger project start
```

This should produce an output that is very similar to the following code:

```
Starting: C:\my-project\app.js...
  project started here: http://localhost:10010/
  project will restart on changes.
  to restart at any time, enter `rs`
try this:
curl http://127.0.0.1:10010/hello?name=Scott
```

Now, if we follow the instructions of the output and execute the curl command, we get the following output:

```
curl http://127.0.0.1:10010/hello?name=David
```

```
"Hello David!"
```

Swagger is binding the `name` query parameter to the Swagger parameter specified in the YAML definition. This may sound bad, as we are coupling our software to Swagger, but it gives you an immense benefit: Swagger allows you to test the endpoint through the editor. Let's see how it works.

On the right-hand side of the editor, you can see a button with the **Try this operation** label, as shown in the following screenshot:

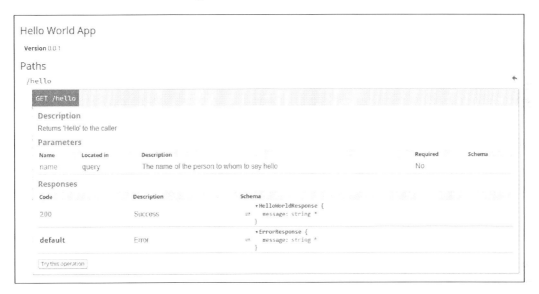

Once you click it, it will present you a form that allows you to test the endpoint, as shown in the following screenshot:

There is a warning message on this form about cross-origin requests. We don't need to worry about it when developing in our local machine; however, we could have problems when testing other hosts using the Swagger Editor.

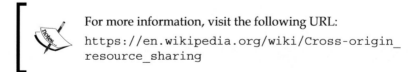 For more information, visit the following URL:
https://en.wikipedia.org/wiki/Cross-origin_resource_sharing

Enter a value for the **name** parameter, and after that, click on **Send Request**, as shown in the following image:

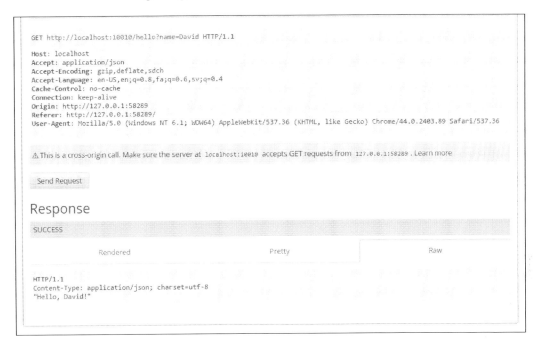

```
GET http://localhost:10010/hello?name=David HTTP/1.1

Host: localhost
Accept: application/json
Accept-Encoding: gzip,deflate,sdch
Accept-Language: en-US,en;q=0.8,fa;q=0.6,sv;q=0.4
Cache-Control: no-cache
Connection: keep-alive
Origin: http://127.0.0.1:58289
Referer: http://127.0.0.1:58289/
User-Agent: Mozilla/5.0 (Windows NT 6.1; WOW64) AppleWebKit/537.36 (KHTML, like Gecko) Chrome/44.0.2403.89 Safari/537.36


⚠ This is a cross-origin call. Make sure the server at localhost:10010 accepts GET requests from 127.0.0.1:58289. Learn more

Send Request
```

Response

SUCCESS

| Rendered | Pretty | Raw |

```
HTTP/1.1
Content-Type: application/json; charset=utf-8
"Hello, David!"
```

This is a response example using Swagger Editor to test the endpoint

Be aware that, for this test to work, our app server has to be up and running.

Generating a project from the Swagger definition

Until now, we have been playing with Swagger and the generated project, but we are now going to generate the project from the `swagger.yaml` file. We will use the already generated project as a starting point, but we will add a new endpoint:

```
swagger: "2.0"
info:
  version: "0.0.1"
  title: Stop Words Filtering App
host: localhost:8000
basePath: /
schemes:
  - http
  - https
```

```
consumes:
  - application/json
produces:
  - application/json
paths:
  /stop-words:
    x-swagger-router-controller: stop_words
    get:
      description: Removes the stop words from an arbitrary input
        text.
      operationId: stopwords
      parameters:
        - name: text
          in: query
          description: The text to be sanitized
          required: false
          type: string
      responses:
        "200":
          description: Success
          schema:
            $ref: "#/definitions/StopWordsResponse"
  /swagger:
    x-swagger-pipe: swagger_raw
definitions:
  StopWordsResponse:
    required:
      - message
    properties:
      message:
        type: string
```

This endpoint might sound very familiar to you, as we unit tested it earlier in this chapter. As you probably know by now, the Swagger Editor is quite cool: it provides feedback as you type on, about what is going on in the YAML file, as well as saves the changes.

The next step is to download the Swagger code generator from https://github. com/swagger-api/swagger-codegen. It is a Java project, so we are going to need the Java SDK and Maven to build it, as follows:

```
mvn package
```

Codegen is a tool that allow us to read the API definition from the Swagger YAML and build the basic structure for a project in a language of our choice, in this case, Node.js.

The preceding command in the root of the project should build all the submodules. Now, it is as easy as executing the following command in the root of the swagger-codegen folder:

```
java -jar modules/swagger-codegen-cli/target/swagger-codegen-cli.jar
generate -i my-project.yaml -l nodejs -o my-project
```

The Swagger code generator supports a number of languages. Here, the trick is that when using it for microservices, we can define the interface and then use the most appropriate technology to build our service.

If you go to the my-project folder, you should find the full structure of the project in there, ready to start coding.

Summary

In this chapter, you learned how to test and document microservices. It is usually the forgotten activity in software development, due to the pressures to deliver new functionalities, but in my opinion, it is a risky decision. We have to find the balance between too much and very little testing. In general, we will always try to find the right proportion for unit, integration and end-to-end tests.

You also learned about manual testing and the tools to efficiently test our software manually (there is always a component of manual testing).

Another interesting point is the documentation and API management. In this case, we got to know Swagger, which is probably the most popular API manager that led to the creation of the Open API standard.

If you want to go deeper in to the API world (there is a lot to learn in order to build a practical and efficient API), you should probably browse http://apigee.com. Apigee are a company expert on building APIs and providing tools for developers and enterprises that could help you to build a better API.

7
Monitoring Microservices

Monitoring servers is always a controversial subject. It usually falls under system administration, and software engineers don't even go near it, but we are losing one of the huge benefits of monitoring: *the ability to react quickly to failures*. By monitoring our system very closely, we can be aware of problems almost immediately so that the actions to correct the problem may even save us from impacting the customers. Along with monitoring, there is the concept of performance. By knowing how our system behaves during load periods, we will be able to anticipate the necessity of scaling the system. In this chapter, we will discuss how to monitor servers, and specifically microservices, in order to maintain the stability of our system.

In this chapter, we will cover the following topics:

- Monitoring services
- Monitoring using PM2 and Keymetrics
- Monitoring metrics
- Simian Army – the active monitoring from Spotify
- Throughput and performance degradation

Monitoring services

When monitoring a microservice, we are interested in a few different types of metrics. The first big group of metrics is the hardware resources, which are described as follows:

- **Memory metrics**: This indicates how much memory is left in our system or consumed by our application
- **CPU utilization**: As the name suggests, this indicates how much CPU are we using at a given time
- **Disk utilization**: This indicates the I/O pressure in the physical hard drives

The second big group is the application metrics, as follows:

- Number of errors per time unit
- Number of calls per time unit
- Response time

Even though both groups are connected and a problem in the hardware will impact the application performance (and the other way around), knowing all of them is a must.

Hardware metrics are easy to query if our server is a Linux machine. On Linux, all the magic of hardware resources happens in the /proc folder. This folder is maintained by the kernel of the system and contains files about how the system behaves regarding a number of aspects in the system.

Software metrics are harder to collect and we are going to use **Keymetrics** from the creators of PM2 to monitor our Node.js applications.

Monitoring using PM2 and Keymetrics

PM2, as we've seen before, is a very powerful instrument to run Node applications, but it is also very good at monitoring standalone applications in production servers. However, depending on your business case, it is not always easy to get access to the production.

The creators of PM2 have solved this problem by creating Keymetrics. Keymetrics is a **Software as a service (SaaS)** component that allows PM2 to send monitoring data across the network to its website, as shown in the following image (as found at https://keymetrics.io/):

Even though Keymetrics is not free, it provides a free tier to demonstrate how it works. We are going to use it in this chapter.

The very first thing that we need to do is register a user. Once we get access to our account, we should see something similar to the following screen:

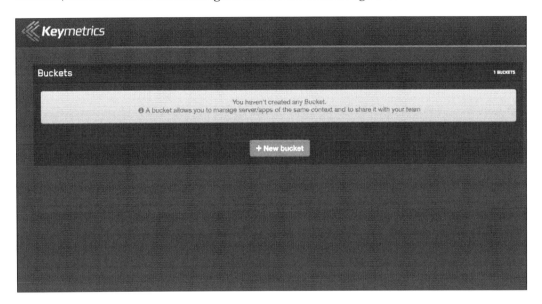

This screen is asking us to create a bucket. Keymetrics uses the bucket concept to define a context. For example, if our organization has different areas (payments, customer service, and so on) with different servers on each area, we could monitor all the servers in one bucket. There are no restrictions on how many servers you can have in one bucket. It is even possible to have all the organization in the same bucket so that everything is easy to access.

Let's create a bucket called Monitoring Test, as shown in the following image:

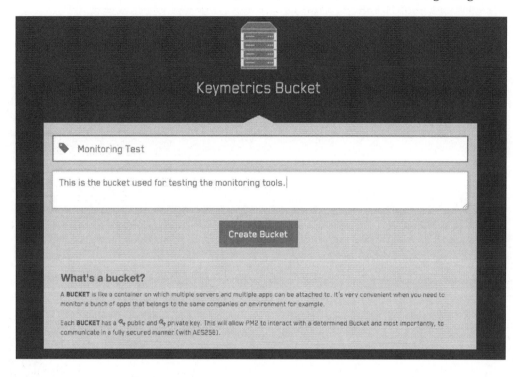

Easy, once we tap on **Create Bucket**, Keymetrics will show us a screen with the information needed to start monitoring our app, as shown in the following image:

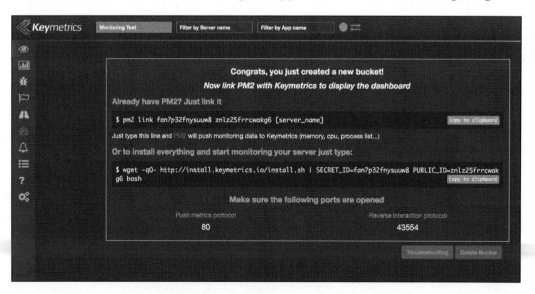

As you can see, the screen displays information about the private key used by Keymetrics. Usually, it is a very bad idea to share this key with anyone.

As shown on the screen, the next step is to configure PM2 to push data into Keymetrics. There is also useful information about the networking needed to make Keymetrics work:

- PM2 will be pushing data to the port **80** on Keymetrics
- Keymetrics will be pushing data back to us on the port **43554**

Usually, in large organizations, there are restrictions about the networking, but if you are testing this from home, everything should work straightaway.

In order to make PM2 able to send metrics to Keymetrics, we need to install one PM2 module called `pm2-server-monit`. This is a fairly easy task:

```
pm2 install pm2-server-monit
```

This will result in an output similar to the following:

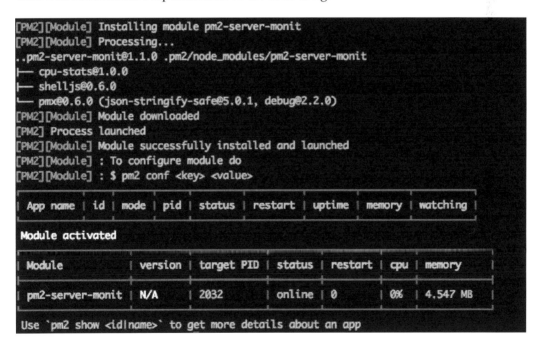

Let's run the advised command:

```
pm2 link fan7p32fnysuuw8 znlz25frrcwakg6 my-server
```

In this case, I have replaced [server name] with my-server. There are no restrictions on the server name; however, when rolling out Keymetrics into a real system, it is recommended to choose a descriptive name in order to easily identify the server in the dashboard.

The preceding command will produce an output similar to the following image:

```
[Keymetrics.io] Using (Public key: znlz25frrcwakg6) (Private key:
fan7p32fnysuuw8)
[Keymetrics.io] [Agent created] Agent ACTIVE - Web Access:
https://app.keymetrics.io/
```

This is an indication that everything went well and our application is ready to be monitored from Keymetrics that can be checked on https://app.keymetrics.io/, as follows:

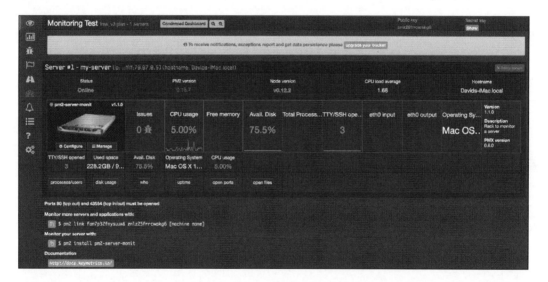

Now, our server is showing up in the interface. As we previously stated, this bucket could monitor different servers. A simple virtual machine is created, and as you can see at the bottom of the screen, Keymetrics provides us with the command to be executed in order to add another server. In this case, as we are using the free access to Keymetrics, so we can only monitor one server.

Let's see what Keymetrics can offer us. At first sight, we can see interesting metrics such as CPU usage, memory available, disk available, and so on.

All these are hardware metrics that indicate how our system is behaving. Under pressure, they are the perfect indicator to point out the need for more hardware resources.

Usually, the hardware resources are the main indicator of failure in an application. Now, we are going to see how to use Keymetrics to diagnose the problem.

Diagnosing problems

A memory leak is usually a difficult problem to solve due to the nature of the flaw. Take a look at the following code.

Let's run the program using a simple `seneca.act()` action:

```
var seneca = require('seneca')();

var names = [];

seneca.add({cmd: 'memory-leak'}, function(args, done){
  names.push(args.name);
  greetings = "Hello " + args.name;
  done(null ,{result: greetings});
});

seneca.act({cmd: 'memory-leak', name: 'David'}, function(err,
  response) {
  console.log(response);
});
```

This program has a very obvious memory leak, and by obvious, I mean that it is written to be obvious. The `names` array will keep growing indefinitely. In the preceding example, it is not a big deal due to the fact that our application is a script that will start and finish without keeping the state in memory.

> Remember that JavaScript allocates variables in the global scope if the `var` keyword is not used.

The problem comes when someone else reutilizes our code in a different part of the application.

Let's assume that our system grows to a point that we need a microservice to greet new customers (or deliver the initial payload of personal information such as name, preferences, configuration, and so on). The following code could be a good example on how to build it:

```
var seneca = require('seneca')();

var names = [];

seneca.add({cmd: 'memory-leak'}, function(args, done){
  names.push(args.name);
  greetings = "Hello " + args.name;
  done(null ,{result: greetings});
});

seneca.listen(null, {port: 8080});
```

In this example, Seneca will be listening over HTTP for requests from Seneca clients or other types of systems such as **curl**. When we run the application:

```
node index.js
```

```
2016-02-14T13:30:26.748Z szwj2mazorea/1455456626740/40489/- INFO hello
Seneca/1.1.0/szwj2mazorea/1455456626740/40489/-
```

```
2016-02-14T13:30:27.003Z szwj2mazorea/1455456626740/40489/- INFO listen
{port:8080}
```

Then from another terminal, we use curl to act as a client of our microservice, everything will work smoothly and our memory leak will go unnoticed:

```
curl -d '{"cmd": "memory-leak", "name":"David"}' http://127.0.0.1:8080/
act
```

```
{"result":"Hello David"}%
```

However, we are going to use Keymetrics to find the problem. The first thing we need to do is run our program using PM2. In order to do it so, we run the following command:

```
pm2 start index.js
```

This command will produce the following output:

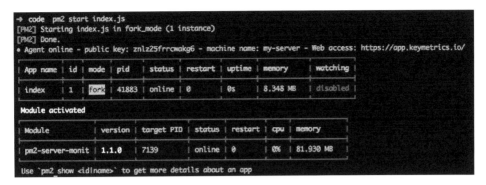

Let's explain the output in the following:

- The first line gives us information about the integration with Keymetrics. Data such as public key, server name, and the URL to access Keymetrics.

- In the first table, we can see the name of the application running, as well as few statistics on memory, uptime, CPU, and so on.

- In the second table, we can see the information relevant to the `pm2-server-monit` PM2 module.

Now, let's go to Keymetrics and see what has happened:

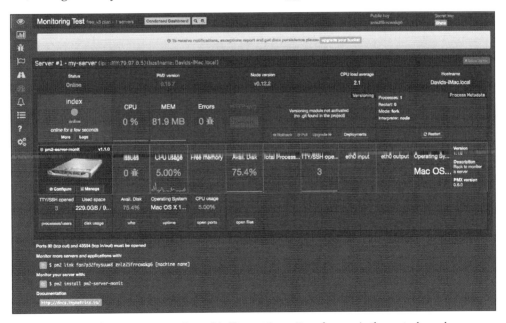

The application is now registered in Keymetrics as it can be seen in the control panel

As you can see, now our application is showing up in Keymetrics.

Straightaway, we can see the very useful things about our app. One of these is the memory used. This is the metric that will indicate a memory leak, as it will keep growing.

Now, we are going to force the memory leak to cause a problem in our application. In this case, the only thing that we need to do is start our server (the small application that we wrote before) and issue a significant number of requests:

```
for i in {0..100000}
do
  curl -d '{"cmd": "memory-leak", "name":"David"}'
    http://127.0.0.1:8080/act
done
```

As simple as the small bash script, this is all it takes to open Pandora's Box in our application:

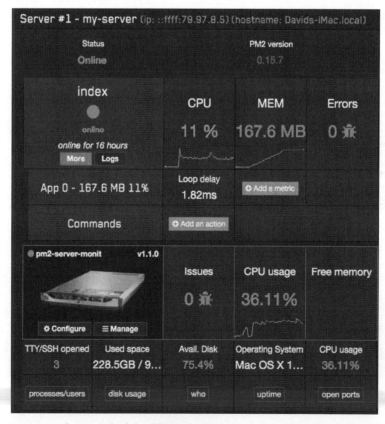

The application is now showing a high load (36% of CPU and an increased use of memory up to 167 MB)

The preceding image shows the impact of running the loop of requests in our system. Let's explain it in the following:

- The CPU in our application has gone to **11%** with an average loop delay of **1.82** milliseconds. Regarding our system, the overall CPU utilization has gone up to **36.11%** due to the fact that both the application and bash script use a significant amount of resources.

- The memory consumption has soared from **81.9 MB** to **167.6 MB**. As you can see, the line on the graph of memory allocation is not going straight up, and that is due to garbage collections. A garbage collection is an activity within the Node.js framework where unreferenced objects are freed from the memory, allowing our system to reuse the hardware resources.

- Regarding the errors, our application has been stable with **0** errors (we'll come back to this section later).

Now, once our bash script is finished (I stopped it manually, as it can take a significant amount of resources and time to finish), we can again see what happened to our system in the following screenshot:

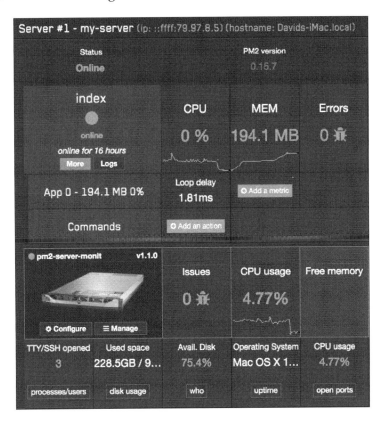

We can see that the CPU has gone back to normal, but what about the memory? The memory consumed by our application hasn't been freed due to the fact that our program has a memory leak, and as long as our variable is referencing the memory consumed (remember the names array is accumulating more and more names), it won't be freed.

In this case, we have a very simple example that clearly shows where the memory leak is, but in complex applications, it is not always obvious. This error, in particular, could never show up as a problem due to the fact that we probably deploy new versions of our app often enough to not realize it.

Monitoring application exceptions

Application errors are events that occur when our application can't handle an unexpected situation. Things such as dividing a number by zero or trying to access an undefined property of our application usually leads to these type of problems.

When working on a multithreaded framework (language) such as Tomcat, the fact that one of our threads dies due to an exception usually only affects to one customer (the one holding the thread). However, in Node.js, a bubbled exception could be a significant problem as our application dies.

PM2 and Seneca do a very good job at keeping it alive as PM2 will restart our app if something makes it stop, and Seneca won't let the application die if an exception occurs in one of the actions.

Keymetrics has developed a module called **pmx** that we can use to programmatically get alerts on errors:

```
var seneca = require('seneca')();

var pmx = require('pmx');

var names = [];

seneca.add({cmd: 'exception'}, function(args, done){
  pmx.notify(new Error("Unexpected Exception!"));

  done(null ,{result: 100/args.number});
});

seneca.listen({port: 8085});
```

It is easy and self-descriptive: an action that sends an exception to Keymetrics if the number sent as a parameter is zero. If we run it, we will get the following output:

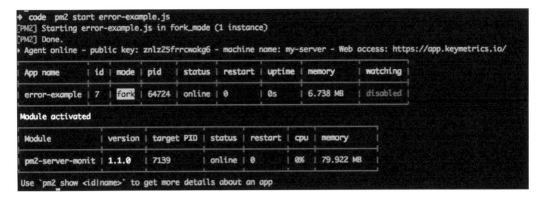

Now we need to hit the server in order to cause the error. As we did earlier, we will do this using curl:

```
curl -d '{"cmd": "exception", "number": "0"}' http://localhost:8085/act
{"result":null}%
```

Now, when we go to Keymetrics, we can see that there is an error logged, as shown in the following image:

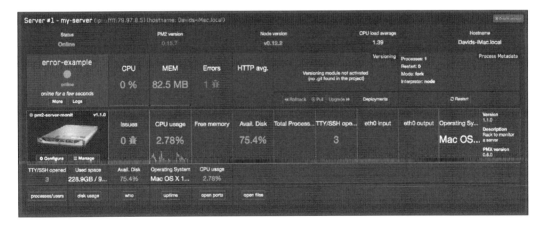

Another interesting point of Keymetrics is the configuration of alerts. As PM2 sends data about pretty much every metric in our system, we have the ability to configure Keymetrics on the thresholds that we consider healthy for our application.

This is very handy as we could get the notifications integrated in our corporate chat (something similar to **Slack**) and be alerted real time when something is not going correctly in our application.

Custom metrics

Keymetrics also allows us to use **probes**. A probe is a custom metric that is sent programmatically by the application to Keymetrics.

There are different types of values that the native library from Keymetrics allows us to push directly. We are going to see the most useful ones.

Simple metric

A simple metric is, as its name indicates, a very basic metric where the developer can set the value to the data sent to Keymetrics:

```
var seneca = require('seneca')();
var pmx = require("pmx").init({
  http: true,
  errors: true,
  custom_probes: true,
  network: true,
  ports: true
});
var names = [];
var probe = pmx.probe();

var meter = probe.metric({
  name       : 'Last call'
});

seneca.add({cmd: 'last-call'}, function(args, done){
  console.log(meter);
  meter.set(new Date().toISOString());
  done(null, {result: "done!"});
});

seneca.listen({port: 8085});
```

In this case, the metric will send the time when the action was called for the last time to the Keymetrics:

The configuration for this metric is non-existent:

```
var probe = pmx.probe();

var meter = probe.metric({
    name       : 'Last call'
});
```

There is no complexity in this metric.

Counter

This metric is very useful to count how many times an event occurred:

```
var seneca = require('seneca')();
var pmx = require("pmx").init({
    http: true,
    errors: true,
    custom_probes: true,
    network: true,
    ports: true
});
var names = [];
var probe = pmx.probe();

var counter = probe.counter({
    name : 'Number of calls'
});

seneca.add({cmd: 'counter'}, function(args, done){
    counter.inc();
    done(null, {result: "done!"});
});

seneca.listen({port: 8085});
```

In the preceding code, we can see how the counter is incremented for every single call to the action counter.

This metric will also allow us to decrement the value calling the `dec()` method on the counter:

```
counter.dec();
```

Average calculated values

This metric allows us to record when an event occurs, and it will automatically calculate the number of events per time unit. It is quite useful to calculate averages and is a good tool to measure the load in the system. Let's see a simple example, as follows:

```
var seneca = require('seneca')();
var pmx = require("pmx").init({
   http: true,
   errors: true,
   custom_probes: true,
   network: true,
   ports: true
});
var names = [];
var probe = pmx.probe();

var meter = probe.meter({
   name       : 'Calls per minute',
   samples    : 60,
   timeframe  : 3600
});

seneca.add({cmd: 'calls-minute'}, function(args, done){
   meter.mark();
   done(null, {result: "done!"});
});

seneca.listen({port: 8085});
```

The preceding code creates a probe and sends a new metric called `Calls per minute` to Keymetrics.

Now, if we run the application and the following command a few times, the metric is shown in the following Keymetrics interface:

```
curl -d '{"cmd": "calls-minute"}' http://localhost:8085/act
```

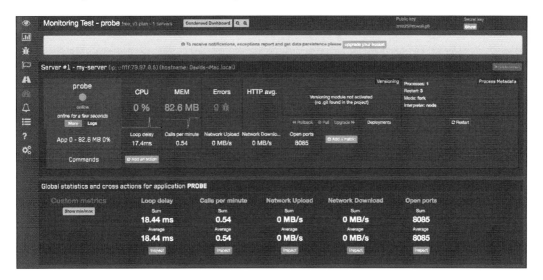

As you can see, there is a new metric called `Calls per minute` in the UI. The key to configure this metric is in the following initialization:

```
var meter = probe.meter({
    name      : 'Calls per minute',
    samples   : 60,
    timeframe : 3600
});
```

As you can see, the name of the metric is in the configuration dictionary as well as in two parameters: `samples` and `timeframe`.

The `samples` parameter correspond to the interval where we want to rate the metric; in this case, it is the number of calls per minute so that rate is `60` seconds.

The `timeframe` parameter, on the other hand, is for how long we want Keymetrics to hold the data for, or to express in simpler words, it is the timeframe over which the metric will be analyzed.

Simian Army – the active monitoring from Spotify

Spotify is one of the companies of reference when building microservices-oriented applications. They are extremely creative and talented when it boils down to coming up with new ideas.

One of my favourite ideas among them is what they call the **Simian Army**. I like to call it **active monitoring**.

In this book, I have talked a lot times about how humans fail at performing different tasks. No matter how much effort you put in to creating your software, there are going to be bugs that will compromise the stability of the system.

This is a big problem, but it becomes a huge deal when, with the modern cloud providers, your infrastructure is automated with a script.

Think about it, what happens if in a pool of thousand servers, three of them have the *time zone out of sync* with the rest of the servers? Well, depending on the nature of your system, it could be fine or it could be a big deal. Can you imagine your bank giving you a statement with disordered transactions?

Spotify has solved (or mitigated) the preceding problem by creating a number of software agents (a program that moves within the different machines of our system), naming them after different species of monkeys with different purposes to ensure the robustness of their infrastructure. Let's explain it a bit further.

As you are probably aware, if you have worked before with Amazon Web Services, the machines and computational elements are divided in to regions (EU, Australia, USA, and so on) and inside every region, there are availability zones, as shown in the following diagram:

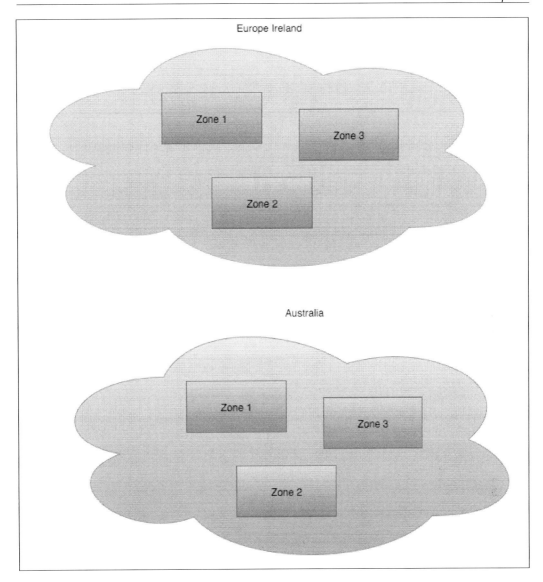

This enables us, the engineers, to create software and infrastructure without hitting what we call a single point of failure.

 A **single point of failure** is a condition in a system where the failure of a single element will cause the system to misbehave.

This configuration raised a number of questions to the engineers in Spotify, as follows:

- What happens if we blindly trust our design without testing whether we actually have any point of failures or not?

- What happens if a full availability zone or region goes down?

- How is our application going to behave if there is an abnormal latency for some reason?

To answer all these questions, Netflix has created various agents. An agent is a software that runs on a system (in this case, our microservices system) and carries on different operations such as checking the hardware, measuring the network latency, and so on. The idea of agent is not new, but until now, its application was nearly a futuristic subject. Let's take a look at the following agents created by Netflix:

- **Chaos Monkey**: This agent disconnects healthy machines from the network in a given availability zone. This ensures that there are *no single points of failures within an availability zone*. So that if our application is balanced across four nodes, when the Chaos Monkey kicks in, it will disconnect one of these four machines.

- **Chaos Gorilla**: This is similar to Chaos Monkey, Chaos Gorilla will disconnect a full availability zone in order to verify that Netflix services rebalance to the other available zones. In other words, Chaos Gorilla is the big brother of Chaos Monkey; instead of operating at the server level, it operates at the partition level.

- **Latency Monkey**: This agent is responsible for introducing artificial latencies in the connections. Latency is usually something that is hardly considered when developing a system, but it is a very delicate subject when building a microservices architecture: latency in one node could compromise the quality of the full system. When a service is running out of resources, usually the first indication is the latency in the responses; therefore, Latency Monkey *is a good way to find out how our system will behave under pressure*.

- **Doctor Monkey**: A health check is an endpoint in our application that returns an HTTP 200 if everything is correct and 500 error code if there is a problem within the application. Doctor Monkey is an agent that will randomly execute the health check of nodes in our application and report the faulty ones in order to replace them.

- **10-18 Monkey**: Organizations such as Netflix are global, so they need to be language-aware (certainly, you don't want to get a website in German when your mother tongue is Spanish). The 10-18 Monkey reports on instances that are misconfigured.

There are a few other agents, but I just want to explain active monitoring to you. Of course, this type of monitoring is out of reach of small organizations, but it is good to know about their existence so that we can get inspired to set up our monitoring procedures.

 The code is available under Apache License in the following repository: `https://github.com/Netflix/SimianArmy`.

In general, this active monitoring follows the philosophy of *fail early*, of which, I am a big adept. No matter how big the flaw in your system is or how critical it is, you want to find it sooner than later, and ideally, without impacting any customer.

Throughput and performance degradation

Throughput is to our application what the monthly production is to a factory. It is a unit of measurement that gives us an indication about how our application is performing and answers the *how many* question of a system.

Very close to throughput, there is another unit that we can measure: **latency**.

Latency is the performance unit that answers the question of *how long*.

Let's consider the following example:

Our application is a microservices-based architecture that is responsible for calculating credit ratings of applicants to withdraw a mortgage. As we have a large volume of customers (a nice problem to have), we have decided to process the applications in batches. Let's draw a small algorithm around it:

```
var seneca = require('seneca')();
var senecaPendingApplications = require('seneca').client({type:
  'tcp',
  port: 8002,
  host: "192.168.1.2"});
  var senecaCreditRatingCalculator =
    require('seneca').client({type: 'tcp',
  port: 8002,
  host: "192.168.1.3"});

seneca.add({cmd: 'mortgages', action: 'calculate'}, function(args,
callback) {
  senecaPendingApplications.act({
    cmd: 'applications',
    section: 'mortgages',
```

```
    custmers: args.customers}, function(err, responseApplications) {
      senecaCreditRatingCalculator.act({cmd: 'rating',
        customers: args.customers}, function(err, response) {

        processApplications(response.ratings,
        responseApplications.applications,
        args.customers
      );
    });
  });
});
```

This is a small and simple Seneca application (this is only theoretical, don't try to run it as there is a lot of code missing!) that acts as a client for two other microservices, as follows:

- The first one gets the list of pending applications for mortgages
- The second one gets the list of credit rating for the customers that we have requested

This could be a real situation for processing mortgage applications. In all fairness, I worked on a very similar system in the past, and even though it was a lot more complex, the workflow was very similar.

Let's talk about throughput and latency. Imagine that we have a fairly big batch of mortgages to process and the system is misbehaving: the network is not being as fast as it should and is experiencing some dropouts.

Some of these applications will be lost and will need to be retried. In ideal conditions, our system is producing a throughput of 500 applications per hour and takes an average of 7.2 seconds on latency to process every single application. However, today, as we stated before, the system is not at its best; we are processing only 270 applications per hour and takes on average 13.3 seconds to process a single mortgage application.

As you can see, with latency and throughput, we can measure how our business transactions are behaving with respect to the previous experiences; we are operating at 54% of our normal capacity.

This could be a serious issue. In all fairness, a drop off like this should ring all the alarms in our systems as something really serious is going on in our infrastructure; however, if we have been smart enough while building our system, the performance will be degraded, but our system won't stop working. This can be easily achieved by the usage of circuit breakers and queueing technologies such as **RabbitMQ**.

Queueing is one of the best examples to show how to apply human behavior to an IT system. Seriously, the fact that we can easily decouple our software components having a simple message as a joint point, which our services either produce or consume, gives us a big advantage when writing complex software.

Other advantage of queuing over HTTP is that an HTTP message is lost if there is a network drop out.

We need to build our application around the fact that it is either full success or error. With queueing technologies such as RabbitMQ, our messaging delivery is asynchronous so that we don't need to worry about intermittent failures: *as soon as we can deliver the message to the appropriate queue, it will get persisted until the client is able to consume it (or the message timeout occurs).*

This enables us to account for intermittent errors in the infrastructure and build even more robust applications based on the communication around queues.

Again, Seneca makes our life very easy: the plugin system on which the Seneca framework is built makes writing a transport plugin a fairly simple task.

> RabbitMQ transport plugin can be found in the following GitHub repository:
>
> `https://github.com/senecajs/seneca-rabbitmq-transport`
>
> There are quite few transport plugins and we can also create our own ones (or modify the existing ones!) to satisfy our needs.

If you take a quick look at the RabbitMQ plugin (just as an example), the only thing that we need to do to write a transport plugin is overriding the following two Seneca actions:

- `seneca.add({role: 'transport', hook: 'listen', type: 'rabbitmq'}, ...)`
- `seneca.add({role: 'transport', hook: 'client', type: 'rabbitmq'}, ...)`

Using queueing technologies, our system will be *more resilient against intermittent failures* and we would be able to degrade the performance instead of heading into a catastrophic failure due to missing messages.

Summary

In this chapter, we deep dived into PM2 monitoring through Keymetrics. We learned how to put tight monitoring in place so that we are quickly informed about the failures in our application.

In the software development life cycle, the **QA** phase is, in my opinion, one of the most important one: no matter how good your code looks, if it does not work, it is useless. However, if I have to choose another phase where engineers should put more emphasis, it would be the deployment, and more specifically, the monitoring that is carried out after every deployment. If you receive error reports immediately, chances are that the reaction can be quick enough to avoid bigger problems such as corrupted data or customers complaining.

We also saw an example of active monitoring carried out by Netflix on their systems, which even though might be out of the reach of your company, it can spark good ideas and practices in order to monitor your software.

Keymetrics is just an example that fits the bill for Node.js as it is extremely well integrated with PM2, but there are also other good monitoring systems such as **AppDynamics**, or if you want to go for an in-house software, you could use Nagios. The key is being clear about what you need to monitor in the application, and then, find the best provider.

Another two good options for monitoring Node.js apps are StrongLoop and New Relic. They are both on the same line with Keymetrics, but they work better for large-scale systems, especially StrongLoop, which is oriented to applications written in Node.js and oriented to microservices.

8
Deploying Microservices

In this chapter, we are going to deploy microservices. We will use different technologies in order to provide the reader with the knowledge required to choose the right tool for every job. First, we will use PM2 and its deployment capabilities to run applications in remote servers. Then, we will play around Docker, which is one of the most advanced deployment platforms, and the entire ecosystem around containers. In this chapter, we will show how to automate all the deployments as highly as possible.

Concepts in software deployment

Deployments are usually the ugly friend of the **Software Development Life Cycle (SDLC)** party. There is a missing contact point between development and systems administration that DevOps is going to solve in the next few years. The cost of fixing bugs at different stages of SDLC is shown in the following figure:

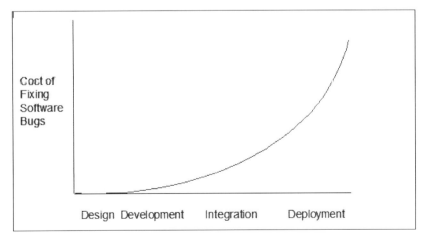

This diagram shows the cost of fixing a bug, depending on the stage of the SDLC

Fail early is one of my favorite concepts in the lean methodology. In the change management world, the cost of fixing a bug in the different stages of the software life cycle is called the **cost of change curve**.

Roughly, fixing a bug in production is estimated to cost 150 times the resources as compared to the costs to fix it when taking requirements.

No matter what the figure is, which depends a lot on the methodology and technology that we use, the lesson learned is that we can save a lot of time by catching bugs early.

From the continuous integration up to continuous delivery, the process should be automated as much as possible, where *as much as possible* means 100%. Remember, humans are imperfect and more prone to errors while carrying out manual repetitive tasks.

Continuous integration

Continuous integration (**CI**) is the practice of integrating the work from different branches on daily basis (or more than once a day) and validating that the changes do not break existing features by running integration and unit tests.

CI should be automated using the same infrastructure configuration as we will be using later in pre-production and production, so if there is any flaw, it can be caught early.

Continuous delivery

Continuous delivery (**CD**) is a software engineering approach that aims to build small, testable, and easily deployable pieces of functionality that can be delivered seamlessly at any time.

This is what we are aiming for with the microservices. Again, we should be pushing to automate the delivery process as, if we are doing it manually, we are only looking for problems.

When talking from the microservices' perspective, automation on deployments is the key. We need to tackle the overhead of having a few dozen of services instead of a few machines, or we can find ourselves maintaining a cloud of services instead of adding value to our company.

Docker is our best ally here. With Docker, we are reducing the hassle of deploying a new software to pretty much moving a file (a container) around in different environments, as we will see later in this chapter.

Deployments with PM2

PM2 is an extremely powerful tool. No matter what stage of development we are in, PM2 always has something to offer.

In this phase of software development, the deployment is where PM2 really shines. Through a JSON configuration file, PM2 will manage a cluster of applications so that we can easily deploy, redeploy, and manage applications on remote servers.

PM2 – ecosystems

PM2 calls a group of applications ecosystem. Every ecosystem is described by a JSON file, and the easiest way to generate it is executing the following command:

```
pm2 ecosystem
```

This should output something similar to the following code:

```
[PM2] Spawning PM2 daemon
[PM2] PM2 Successfully daemonized
File /path/to/your/app/ecosystem.json generated
```

The content of the `ecosystem.json` file varies, depending on the version of PM2, but what this file contains is the skeleton of a PM2 cluster:

```
{
  apps : [

    {
      name      : "My Application",
      script    : "app.js"
    },

    {
      name      : "Test Web Server",
      script    : "proxy-server.js"
    }
  ],

*/
  deploy : {
    production : {
      user : "admin",
      host : "10.0.0.1",
```

```
        ref   : "remotes/origin/master",
        repo : "git@github.com:the-repository.git",
        path : "/apps/repository",
        "post-deploy" : "pm2 startOrRestart ecosystem.json --env
          production"
      },
      dev : {
        user : "devadmin",
        host : "10.0.0.1",
        ref   : "remotes/origin/master",
        repo : "git@github.com:the-repository.git",
        path : "/home/david/development/test-app/",
        "post-deploy" : "pm2 startOrRestart ecosystem.json --env
          dev",
      }
    }
  }
}
```

This file contains two applications configured for two environments. We are going to modify this skeleton to adapt it to our needs, modeling our entire ecosystem written in *Chapter 4, Writing Your First Microservice in Node.js*.

However, for now, let's explain a bit for the configuration:

- We have an array of applications (apps) defining two apps: API and WEB
- As you can see, we have a few configuration parameters for each app:
  - name: This is the name of the application
  - script: This is the startup script of the app
  - env: These are the environment variables to be injected into the system by PM2
  - env_<environment>: This is same as env, but it is tailored per environment

- There are two environments defined in the default ecosystem under the deploy key, as follows:
  - production
  - dev

As you can see, between these two environments, there are no significant changes except for the fact that we are configuring one environment variable in development and the folder where we deploy our application.

Deploying microservices with PM2

In *Chapter 4*, *Writing Your First Microservice in Node.js*, we wrote a simple e-commerce in order to show the different concepts and common catches in microservices.

Now, we are going to learn how to deploy them using PM2.

Configuring the server

First thing we need to do in order to deploy software with PM2 is to configure the remote machine and local machine to be able to talk using SSH, with a public/private key schema.

The way of doing it is easy, as follows:

- Generate one RSA key
- Install it into the remote server

Let's do it:

```
ssh-keygen -t rsa
```

That should produce something similar to the following output:

```
Generating public/private rsa key pair.
Enter file in which to save the key (/Users/youruser/.ssh/id_rsa): /
Users/youruser/.ssh/pm2_rsa
Enter passphrase (empty for no passphrase):
Enter same passphrase again:
Your identification has been saved in pm2_rsa.
Your public key has been saved in pm2_rsa.pub.
The key fingerprint is:
eb:bc:24:fe:23:b2:6e:2d:58:e4:5f:ab:7b:b7:ee:38 dgonzalez@yourmachine.
local
The key's randomart image is:
+--[ RSA 2048]----+
|                 |
|                 |
|                 |
|        .        |
|    o   S        |
|    o   ..       |
```

```
|    o o..o.       |
|   . +.+=E..      |
|   oo++**B+.      |
+-----------------+
```

Now, if we go to the folder indicated in the preceding output, we can find the following two files:

- pm2_rsa: The first one, pm2_rsa, is your private key. As you can read from the name, no one should have access to this key as they may steal your identity in the servers that trust this key.
- pm2_rsa.pub: The pm2_rsa.pub is your public key. This key can be handed over to anyone so that using asymmetric cryptography techniques, they can verify your identity (or who you say you are).

What we are going to do now is copy the public key to the remote server so that when our local machine PM2 tries to talk to the server, it knows who we are and let's get into the shell without password:

```
cat pm2_rsa.pub | ssh youruser@yourremoteserver 'cat >> .ssh/authorized_keys'
```

The last step is to register your private key as a known identity in your local machine:

```
ssh-add pm2_rsa
```

That's about it.

From now on, whenever you SSH into the remote server using as a user youruser, you won't need to enter the password in order to get into the shell.

Once this configuration is done, there is very little to do in order to deploy any application into this server:

```
pm2 deploy ecosystem.json production setup
pm2 deploy ecosystem.json production
```

The first command will configure everything needed to accommodate the app. The second command will actually deploy the application itself as we configured earlier.

Docker – a container for software delivery

Virtualization has been one of the biggest trends in the past few years. Virtualization enables the engineer to share the hardware across different software instances. Docker is not really a virtualization software, but it is conceptually the same.

With a pure virtualization solution, a new OS runs on top of a hypervisor sitting on top of an existing operating system (host OS). Running the full OS means that we can be consuming a few gigabytes of hard drive in order to replicate the full stack from the kernel to the filesystem, which usually consumes a good chunk of resources. The structure of a virtualization solution is shown in the following image:

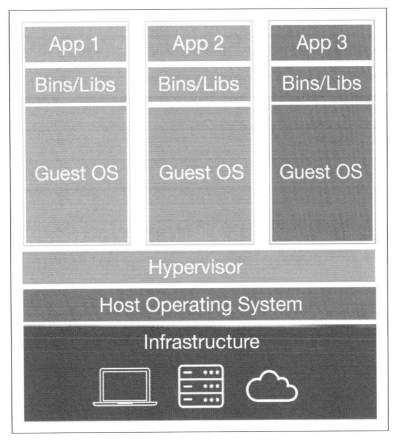

Layers diagram for a virtual machine environment

With Docker, we only replicate the filesystem and binaries so that there is no need to run the full stack of the OS where we don't need it. Docker images are usually a few hundreds of megabytes, instead of gigabytes, and they are quite lightweight, therefore, we can run some containers on the same machine. The previous structure using Docker is shown as follows:

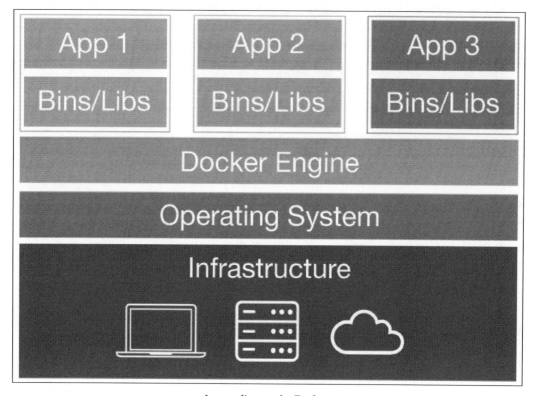

Layers diagram for Docker

With Docker, we also eliminate one of the biggest problems of software deployment, that is, **the configuration management**.

We are switching a complicated per-environment configuration management, where we need to worry about how the application is deployed/configured into a container that is basically like a software package that can be installed in any Docker-ready machine.

The only Docker-ready OS nowadays is Linux, as Docker needs to make use of the advanced kernel features, forcing Windows and Mac users to run a virtual machine with Linux in order to provide support to run Docker containers.

Setting up the container

Docker comes with a very powerful and familiar way (for developers) of configuring the containers.

You can create containers based on an existing image (there are thousands of images on the Internet) and then modify the image to fulfil your needs by adding new software packages or altering the filesystem.

Once we are satisfied with it, we can use the new version of the image to create our containers using a version control system similar to **Git**.

However, we need to understand how Docker works first.

Installing Docker

As it was mentioned before, Docker needs a virtual machine to provide support on Mac and Windows, therefore, the installation on these systems may vary. The best way to install Docker on your system is to go to the official website and follow the steps:

```
https://docs.docker.com/engine/installation/
```

At the moment, it is a very active project, so you can expect changes every few weeks.

Choosing the image

By default, Docker comes with no images. We can verify this by running `docker images` on the terminal, which will produce an output very similar to the following screenshot:

It is an empty list. There are no images stored in the local machine. The first thing we need to do is search for an image. In this case, we are going to use **CentOS** as our base for creating the images. CentOS is very close to Red Hat Enterprise Linux, which seems to be one of the most extended distributions of Linux in the industry. They provide great support and there is plenty of information available on the Internet to troubleshoot problems.

Let's search for a CentOS image as follows:

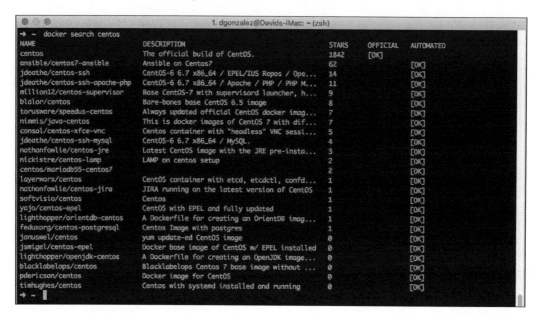

As you can see, there is a long list of images based on CentOS, but only the first one is official.

This list of images is coming from something called the **Registry** in the Docker world. A Docker Registry is a simple repository of images available to the general public. You can also run your own Registry in order to prevent your images from going to the general one.

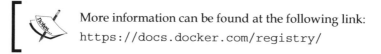

More information can be found at the following link:
`https://docs.docker.com/registry/`

There is one column in the table in the preceding screenshot that should have caught your attention almost immediately, the column called **STARS**. This column represents the rating given by the users for a given image. We can narrow the search based on the number of stars that the users have given to an image by using the -s flag.

If you run the following command, you will see a list of images rated with 1000 or more stars:

```
docker search -s 1000 centos
```

Be careful with the images you choose, there is nothing
preventing a user to create an image with malicious software.

In order to fetch the CentOS image to the local machine, we need to run the
following command:

```
docker pull centos
```

The output produced will be very similar to the following image:

```
➜  ~ docker pull centos
Using default tag: latest
latest: Pulling from library/centos

fa5be2806d4c: Pull complete
2bf4902415e3: Pull complete
86bcb57631bd: Pull complete
c8a648134623: Pull complete
Digest: sha256:8072bc7c66c3d5b633c3fddfc2bf12d5b4c2623f7004d9eed6aae70e0e99fbd7
Status: Downloaded newer image for centos:latest
```

Once the command finishes, if we run Docker images again, we can see that **centos** is
now appearing in the following list:

```
➜  ~ docker images
REPOSITORY          TAG             IMAGE ID        CREATED         VIRTUAL SIZE
centos              latest          c8a648134623    3 weeks ago     196.6 MB
```

As we specified earlier, Docker does not use the full image, but it uses a reduced
version of it, only virtualizing the last few layers of the OS. You can clearly see it, as
the size of the image is not even 200 MB, which for a full version of CentOS, can go
up to a few GB.

Running the container

Now that we have a copy of the image in our local machine, it is time to run it:

```
docker run -i -t centos /bin/bash
```

This will produce the following output:

```
 ➜  ~ docker images
REPOSITORY          TAG             IMAGE ID        CREATED          VIRTUAL SIZE
centos              latest          c8a648134623    3 weeks ago      196.6 MB
 ➜  ~ docker run -i -t centos /bin/bash
[root@debd09c7aa3b /]#
```

As you can see, the prompt of the terminal has changed to something like `root@ debd09c7aa3b`, which means that we are inside the container.

From now on, every single command that we run will be executed inside a contained version of CentOS Linux.

There is another interesting command in Docker:

```
docker ps
```

If we run this command in a new terminal (without exiting from the running container), we will get the following output:

```
 ➜  ~ docker ps
CONTAINER ID     IMAGE        COMMAND         CREATED          STATUS           PORTS           NAMES
62e7336a4627     centos       "/bin/bash"     8 minutes ago    Up 8 minutes                     prickly_bartik
 ➜  ~
```

This output is self explanatory; it is an easy way to see what is going on in our Docker containers.

Installing the required software

Let's install Node.js in the container:

```
curl --silent --location https://rpm.nodesource.com/setup_4.x | bash -
```

This command will pull and execute the setup script for Node.js.

This will produce an output very similar to the following image:

```
[root@0ab9098011c0 /]# curl --silent --location https://rpm.nodesource.com/setup_4.x | bash -

## Installing the NodeSource Node.js 4.x LTS Argon repo...


## Inspecting system...

+ rpm -q --whatprovides redhat-release || rpm -q --whatprovides centos-release || rpm -q --whatprovides cloudlinux-release || rpm -q --whatprovides sl-release
+ uname -m

## Confirming "el7-x86_64" is supported...

+ curl -sLf -o /dev/null 'https://rpm.nodesource.com/pub_4.x/el/7/x86_64/nodesource-release-el7-1.noarch.rpm'

## Downloading release setup RPM...

+ mktemp
+ curl -sL -o '/tmp/tmp.bdco6IfiZY' 'https://rpm.nodesource.com/pub_4.x/el/7/x86_64/nodesource-release-el7-1.noarch.rpm'

## Installing release setup RPM...

+ rpm -i --nosignature --force '/tmp/tmp.bdco6IfiZY'

## Cleaning up...

+ rm -f '/tmp/tmp.bdco6IfiZY'

## Checking for existing installations...

+ rpm -qa 'node|npm' | grep -v nodesource

## Run `yum install -y nodejs` (as root) to install Node.js 4.x LTS Argon and npm.
## You may also need development tools to build native addons:
##   `yum install -y gcc-c++ make`

[root@0ab9098011c0 /]#
```

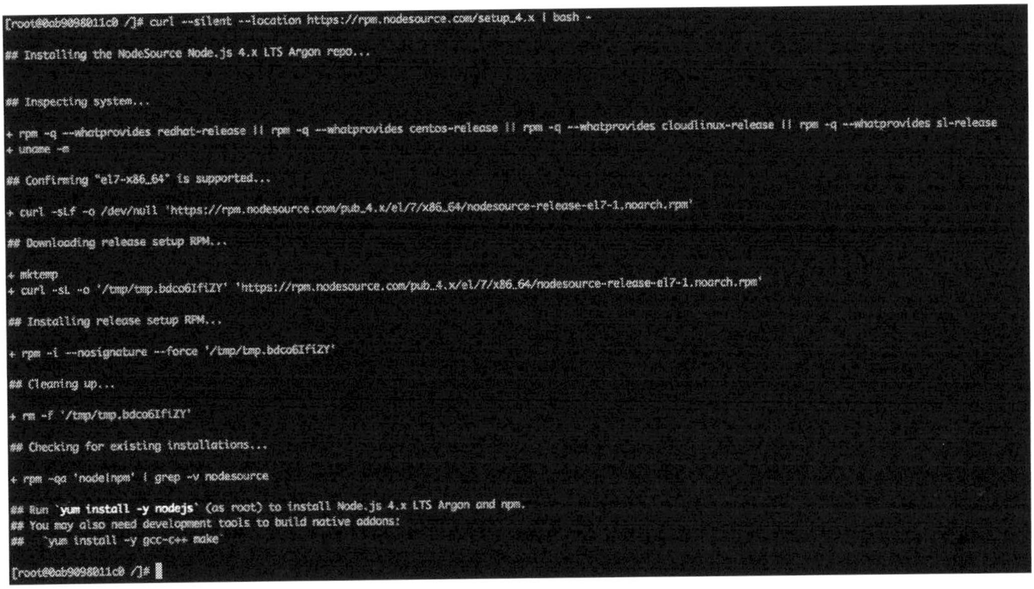

Follow the instructions, as this will install node:

```
yum install -y nodejs
```

It is highly recommended to install the development tools, as the installation process of a few modules requires a compilation step. Let's do it:

```
yum install -y gcc-c++ make
```

Once the command finishes, we are ready to run the node applications inside our container.

Saving the changes

In the Docker world, an image is the configuration for a given container. We can use the image as a template to run as many containers as we want, however first, we need to save the changes made in the previous section.

If you are a software developer, you probably are familiar with control version systems such as CVS, Subversion, or Git. Docker was built with their philosophy in mind—a container can be treated like a versionable software component and then changes can be committed.

In order to do it, run the following command:

```
docker ps -a
```

This command will show a list of containers that have run in the past, as shown in the following image:

```
→ ~ docker ps -a
CONTAINER ID    IMAGE          COMMAND        CREATED           STATUS                       PORTS        NAMES
cf0725a25148    centos         "/bin/bash"    11 seconds ago    Up 10 seconds                             reverent_ritchie
62e7336a4627    centos         "/bin/bash"    15 minutes ago    Exited (0) About a minute ago             prickly_bartik
7bbb50bb7236    centos         "/bin/bash"    16 minutes ago    Exited (0) 16 minutes ago                 jolly_raman
482d0ef324f2    centos         "/bin/bash"    22 minutes ago    Exited (127) 17 minutes ago               adoring_hypatia
debd09c7aa3b    centos         "/bin/bash"    47 hours ago      Exited (137) 24 minutes ago               nostalgic_stallman
ed948a19739b    centos         "/bin/bash"    47 hours ago      Exited (0) 47 hours ago                   jolly_mcclintock
c1f8550c09bb    1d073211c498   "/bin/bash"    10 weeks ago      Exited (0) 10 weeks ago                   fervent_torvalds
```

In my case, there are few containers, but the interesting one in this case is the second; this is where Node.js is installed.

Now, we need to commit the status of the container in order to create a new image with our changes. We do it by running the following command:

```
docker commit -a dgonzalez 62e7336a4627 centos-microservices:1.0
```

Let's explain the command:

- The -a flag indicates the author. In this case, dgonzalez.
- The following parameter is container id. As we indicated earlier, the second container has the corresponding ID 62e7336a4627.
- The third parameter is a combination of the name given to the new image and the tag of the image. The tagging system can be very powerful when we are dealing with quite a few images, as it can get really complicated to identify small variations between them.

It might take a few seconds, but after finishing, the output of the command must be very similar to the following image:

```
→ ~ docker commit -a dgonzalez 62e7336a4627 centos-microservices:1.0
75d9f196b7b4181f41a09163d8177eefcc57649af1ccac9dbcc3af1e2a56bea6
```

This is the indication that we have a new image in our list with our software installed. Run docker images again and the output will confirm it, as shown in the following image:

```
→ ~ docker images
REPOSITORY              TAG        IMAGE ID        CREATED              VIRTUAL SIZE
centos-microservices    1.0        75d9f196b7b4    About a minute ago   306.4 MB
centos                  latest     c8a648134623    3 weeks ago          196.6 MB
```

In order to run a container based on the new image, we can run the following command:

```
docker run -i -t centos-microservices:1.0 /bin/bash
```

This will give us access to the shell in the container, and we can confirm that Node.js is installed by running `node -v`, which should output the version of Node, in this case, 4.2.4.

Deploying Node.js applications

Now, it is time to deploy Node.js applications inside the container. In order to do it, we are going to need to expose the code from our local machine to the Docker container.

The correct way of doing it is by mounting a local folder in the Docker machine, but first, we need to create the small application to be run inside the container, as follows:

```
var express = require('express');
var myApplication = express();

app.get('/hello', function (req, res) {
  res.send('Hello Earth!');
});

var port = 80;

app.listen(port, function () {
  console.log('Listeningistening on port '+ port);
});
```

It is a simple application, using Express that basically renders `Hello Earth!` into a browser. If we run it from a terminal and we access `http://localhost:80/hello`, we can see the results.

Now, we are going to run it inside the container. In order to do it, we are going to mount a local folder as a volume in the Docker container and run it.

Docker comes from the experience of sysadmins and developers that have lately melted into a role called DevOps, which is somewhere in between them. Before Docker, every single company had its own way of deploying apps and managing configurations, so there was no consensus on how to do things the right way.

Now with Docker, the companies have a way to provide uniformity to deployments. No matter what your business is, everything is reduced to build the container, deploy the application, and run the container in the appropriate machine.

Let's assume that the application is in the /apps/test/ folder. Now, in order to expose it to the container, we run the following command:

```
docker run -i -t -v /app/test:/test_app -p 8000:3000 centos-
microservices:1.0 /bin/bash
```

As you can see, Docker can get very verbose with parameters, but let's explain them, as follows:

- The -i and -t flags are familiar to us. They capture the input and send the output to a terminal.

- The -v flag is new. It specifies a volume from the local machine and where to mount it in the container. In this case, we are mounting /apps/test from the local machine into /test_app. Please note the colon symbol to separate the local and the remote path.

- The -p flag specifies the port on the local machine that will expose the remote port in the container. In this case, we expose the port 3000 in the container through the port 8000 in the Docker machine, so accessing docker-machine:8000 from the host machine will end up accessing the port 3000 in the container.

- The centos-microservices:1.0 is the name and tag of the image that we have created in the preceding section.

- The /bin/bash is the command that we want to execute inside the container. The /bin/bash is going to give us access to the prompt of the system.

If everything worked well, we should have gotten access to the system prompt inside the container, as shown in the following image:

```
[root@c079d5f180da /]# cd /test_app/
[root@c079d5f180da test_app]# ls
node_modules  small-script.js
[root@c079d5f180da test_app]#
```

As you can see in the image, there is a folder called /test_app that contains our previous application, called small-script.js.

Now, it is time to access to the app, but first, let's explain how Docker works.

Docker is written in **Go**, which is a modern language created by Google, grouping all the benefits from a compiled language such as C++ with all the high-level features from a modern language such as Java.

It is fairly easy to learn and not hard to master. The philosophy of Go is to bring all the benefits of an interpreted language, such as reducing the compilation times (the complete language can be compiled in under a minute) to a compiled language.

Docker uses very specific features from the Linux kernel that forces Windows and Mac users to use a virtual machine to run Docker containers. This machine used to be called **boot2docker**, but the new version is called **Docker Machine**, which contains more advanced features such as deploying containers in remote virtual machines. For this example, we will only use the local capabilities.

Given that, if you run the app from within the container located in the /test_app/ folder, and you are in Linux, accessing http://localhost:8000/, it would be enough to get into the application.

When you are using Mac or Windows, Docker is running either in the Docker Machine or boot2docker so that the IP is given by this virtual machine, which is shown when the Docker terminal starts, as shown in the following image:

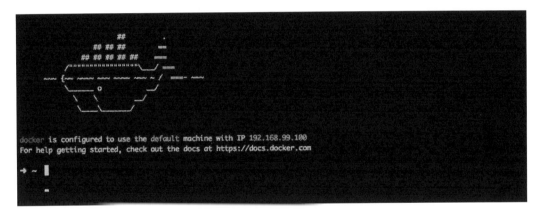

As you can see, the IP is 192.168.99.100, so in order to access our application, we need to visit the http://192.168.99.100:9000/ URL.

Automating Docker container creation

If you remember, in the previous chapters, one of the most important concepts was automation. Automation is the key when working with microservices. Instead of operating one server, you probably will need to operate few dozens, reaching a point where you are almost fully booked on day-to-day tasks.

Docker designers had that in mind when allowing the users to create containers from a script written in a file called `Dockerfile`.

If you have ever worked on coding C or C++, even in college, you are probably familiar with `Makefiles`. A `Makefile` file is a script where the developer specifies the steps to automatically build a software component. Here is an example:

```
all: my-awesome-app

my-awesome-app: main.o external-module.o app-core.o
   g++ main.o external-module.o app-core.o -o my-awesome-app


main.o: main.cc
   g++ -c main.cc


external-module.o: external-module.cc
   g++ -c external-module.cc


app-core.o: app-core.cc
   g++ -c hello.cc

clean:
   rm *.o my-awesome-app
```

The preceding `Makefile` contains a list of tasks and dependencies to be executed. For example, if we execute `make clean` on the same folder where the `Makefile` file is contained, it will remove the executable and all the files ending with `o`.

`Dockerfile`, unlike `Makefile`, is not a list of tasks and dependencies (even though the concept is the same), it is a list of instructions to build a container from scratch to a ready status.

Let's see an example:

```
FROM centos
MAINTAINER David Gonzalez
RUN curl --silent --location https://rpm.nodesource.com/setup_4.x | bash
-
RUN yum -y install nodejs
```

These small few preceding lines are enough to build a container having Node.js installed.

Let's explain it in the following:

- First, we choose the base image. In this case, it is `centos` as we used before. For doing this, we use the `FROM` command and then the name of the image.

- `MAINTAINER` specifies the name of the person who created the container. In this case, it is `David Gonzalez`.

- `RUN`, as its name indicates, runs a command. In this case, we use it twice: once to add the repository to `yum`, and then to install Node.js.

Dockerfiles can contain a number of different commands. The documentation for them is pretty clear, but let's take a look at the most common (aside from the ones seen before):

- `CMD`: This is similar to run, but it actually gets executed after building the command. `CMD` is the command to be used to start an application once the container is instantiated.

- `WORKDIR`: This is to be used in conjunction with `CMD`, it is the command used to specify the work directory for the next `CMD` command.

- `ADD`: This command is used to copy files from the local filesystem to the container instance filesystem. In the previous example, we can use `ADD` to copy the application from the host machine into the container, run `npm install` with the `CMD` command, and then run the app once again with the `CMD` command. It can also be used to copy the content from a URL to a destination folder inside the container.

- `ENV`: This is used to set environment variables. For example, you could specify a folder to store files uploaded by passing an environment variable to the container, as follows:

```
ENV UPLOAD_PATH=/tmp/
```

- `EXPOSE`: This is used to expose ports to the rest of the containers in your cluster.

As you can see, the **domain-specific language (DSL)** of `Dockerfiles` is quite rich and you can pretty much build every system required. There are hundreds of examples on the Internet to build pretty much everything: MySQL, MongoDB, Apache servers, and so on.

It is strongly recommended to create containers through `Dockerfiles`, as it can be used as a script to replicate and make changes to the containers in the future, as well as being able to automatically deploy our software without much manual intervention.

Node.js event loop – easy to learn and hard to master

We all know that Node.js is a platform that runs applications in a single-threaded way; so, why don't we use multiple threads to run applications so that we can get the benefit of multicore processors?

Node.js is built upon a library called **libuv**. This library abstracts the system calls, providing an asynchronous interface to the program that uses it.

I come from a very heavy Java background, and there, everything is synchronous (unless you are coding with some sort of non-blocking libraries), and if you issue a request to the database, the thread is blocked and resumed once the database replies with the data.

This usually works fine, but it presents an interesting problem: a blocked thread is consuming resources that could be used to serve other requests. The event loop of Node.js is shown in the following figure:

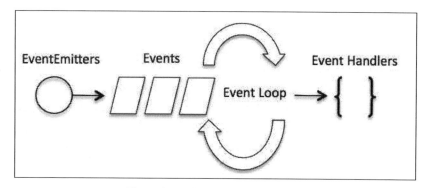

This is the Node.js event loop diagram

JavaScript is, by default, an event-driven language. It executes the program that configures a list of event handlers that will react to given events, and after that, it just waits for the action to take place.

Let's take a look at a very familiar example:

```html
<div id="target">
   Click here
</div>
<div id="other">
   Trigger the handler
</div>
```

Then the JavaScript code is as follows:

```
$( "#target" ).click(function() {
  alert( "Handler for .click() called." );
});
```

As you can see, this is a very simple example. HTML that shows a button and snippet of JavaScript code that, using JQuery, shows an alert box when the button is clicked.

This is the key: *when the button is clicked.*

Clicking a button is an event, and the event is processed through the event loop of JavaScript using a handler specified in the JavaScript.

At the end of the day, we only have one thread executing the events, and we never talk about parallelism in JavaScript, the correct word is concurrency. So, being more concise, we can say that Node.js programs are highly concurrent.

Your application will always be executed in only one thread, and we need to keep that in mind while coding.

If you have been working in Java or .NET or any other language/frameworks designed and implemented with thread-blocking techniques, you might have observed that Tomcat, when running an application, spawns a number of threads listening to the requests.

In the Java world, each of these threads are called **workers**, and they are responsible to handle the request from a given user from the beginning to the end. There is one type of data structure in Java that takes the benefit of it. It is called **ThreadLocal** and it stores the data in the local thread so that it can be recovered later on. This type of storage is possible because the thread that starts the request is also responsible to finish it, and if the thread is executing any blocking operation (such as reading a file or accessing a database), it will wait until it is completed.

This is usually not a big deal, but when your software relies heavily on I/O, the problems can become serious.

Another big point in favor of the non-blocking model of Node.js is the lack of context switch.

When the CPU switches one thread with another, what happens is that all the data in the registers, and other areas of the memory, is stacked and allows the CPU to switch the context with a new process that has its own data to be placed in there, as shown in the following image:

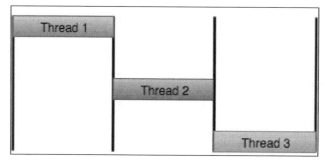

This is a diagram showing context switching in threads from the theoretical point of view.

This operation takes time, and this time is not used by the application. It simply gets lost. In Node.js, your application runs in only one thread, so there is no such context switching while running (it is still present in the background, but hidden to your program). In the following image, we can see what happens in the real world when a CPU switches a thread:

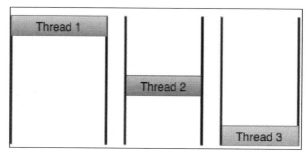

This is a diagram showing context switching in threads from the practical (shows the dead times) point of view.

Clustering Node.js applications

By now, you know how Node.js applications work, and certainly, some of the readers may have a question that if the app runs on a single thread, then what happens with the modern multicore processors?

Before answering this question, let's take a look at the following scenario.

When I was in high school, there was a big technology leap in CPUs: the segmentation.

It was the first attempt to introduce parallelism at the instruction level. As you probably are aware, the CPU interprets assembler instructions and each of these instructions are composed of a number of phases, as shown in the following diagram:

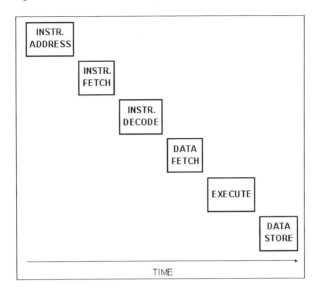

Before the Intel 4x86, the CPUs were executing one instruction at the time, so taking the instruction model from the preceding diagram, any CPU could only execute one instruction every six CPU cycles.

Then, the segmentation came into play. With a set of intermediate registers, the CPU engineers managed to parallelize the individual phases of instructions so that in the best-case scenario, the CPUs are able to execute one instruction per cycle (or nearly), as shown in the following diagram:

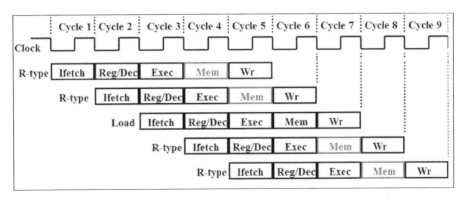

The image describes the execution of instructions in a CPU with a segmented pipeline

This technical improvement led to faster CPUs and opened the door to native hardware multithreading, which led to the modern n-core processors that can execute a large number of parallel tasks, but when we are running Node.js applications, we only use one core.

If we don't cluster our app, we are going to have a serious performance degradation when compared to other platforms that take the benefit of the multiple cores of a CPU.

However, this time we are lucky, PM2 already allows you to cluster Node.js apps to maximize the usage of your CPUs.

Also, one of the important aspects of PM2 is that it allows you to scale applications without any downtime.

Let's run a simple app in the cluster mode:

```
var http = require("http");
http.createServer(function (request, response) {
  response.writeHead(200, {
    'Content-Type': 'text/plain'
  });
  response.write('Here we are!')
  response.end();
}).listen(3000);
```

This time we have used the native HTTP library for Node.js in order to handle the incoming HTTP requests.

Now we can run the application from the terminal and see how it works:

```
node app.js
```

Although it does not output anything, we can curl to the `http://localhost:3000/` URL in order to see how the server responds, as shown in the following screenshot:

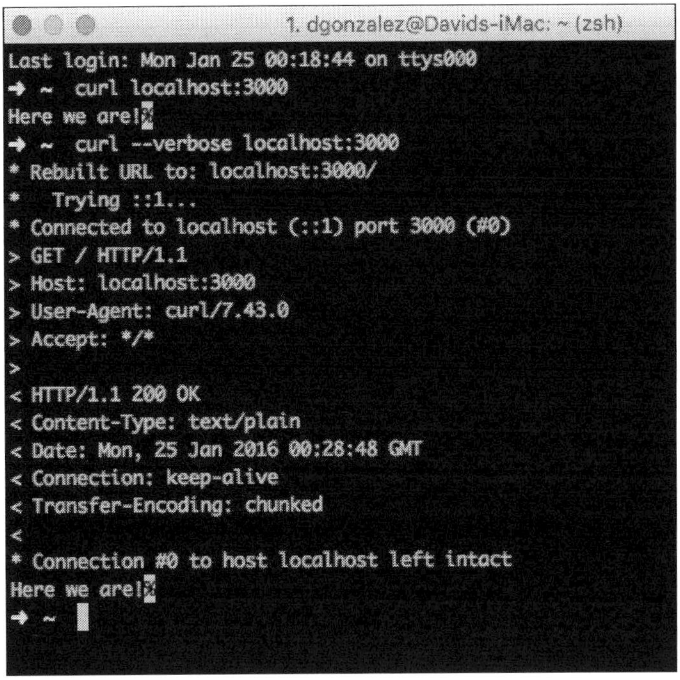

As you can see, Node.js has managed all the HTTP negotiation and it has also managed to reply with the `Here we are!` phrase as it was specified in the code.

This service is quite trivial, but it is the principle on which more complex web services work, so we need to cluster the web service to avoid bottlenecks.

Node.js has one library called `cluster` that allows us to programmatically cluster our application, as follows:

```
var cluster = require('cluster');
var http = require('http');
var cpus = require('os').cpus().length;

// Here we verify if the we are the master of the cluster: This is
  the root process
// and needs to fork al the childs that will be executing the web
  server.
if (cluster.isMaster) {
  for (var i = 0; i < cpus; i++) {
    cluster.fork();
```

```
    }

    cluster.on('exit', function (worker, code, signal) {
      console.log("Worker " + worker.proces.pid + " has finished.");
    });
  } else {
    // Here we are on the child process. They will be executing the
      web server.
    http.createServer(function (request, response) {
      response.writeHead(200);
      response.end('Here we are!d\n');
    }).listen(80);
  }
```

Personally, I find it much easier to use specific software such as PM2 to accomplish effective clustering, as the code can get really complicated while trying to handle the clustered instances of our app.

Given this, we can run the application through PM2 as follows:

pm2 start app.js -i 1

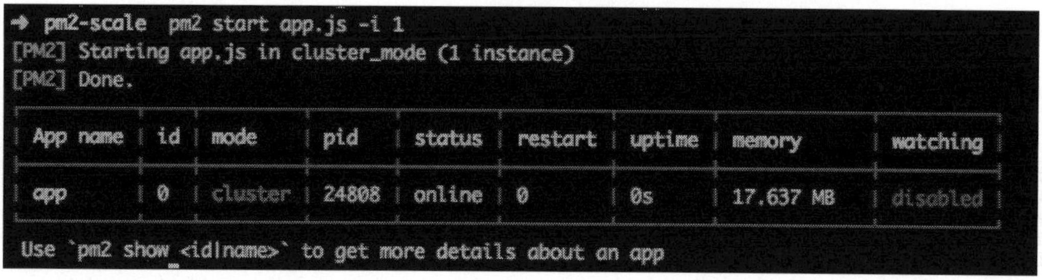

The -i flag in PM2, as you can see in the output of the command, is used to specify the number of cores that we want to use for our application.

If we run pstree, we can see the process tree in our system and check whether PM2 is running only one process for our app, as shown in the following image:

In this case, we are running the app in only one process, so it will be allocated in one core of the CPU.

In this case, we are not taking advantage of the multicore capabilities of the CPU that is running the app, but we still get the benefit of restarting the app automatically if one exception bubbles up from our algorithm.

Now, we are going to run our application using all the cores available in our CPU so that we maximize the usage of it, but first, we need to stop the cluster:

```
pm2 stop all
```

```
➜  ~  pm2 stop all
[PM2] Stopping all
[PM2] stopProcessId process id 0
```

App name	id	mode	pid	status	restart	uptime	memory	watching
app	0	cluster	0	stopped	0	0	0 B	disabled

```
Use `pm2 show <id|name>` to get more details about an app
```

PM2, after stopping all the services

```
pm2 delete all
```

Now, we are in a position to rerun the application using all the cores of our CPU:

```
pm2 start app.js -i 0
```

```
➜  pm2-scale  pm2 start app.js -i 0
[PM2] Starting app.js in cluster_mode (0 instance)
[PM2] Done.
```

App name	id	mode	pid	status	restart	uptime	memory	watching
app	0	cluster	25033	online	0	0s	26.156 MB	disabled
app	1	cluster	25034	online	0	0s	25.941 MB	disabled
app	2	cluster	25035	online	0	0s	26.053 MB	disabled
app	3	cluster	25036	online	0	0s	19.305 MB	disabled

```
Use `pm2 show <id|name>` to get more details about an app
```

PM2 showing four services running in a cluster mode

PM2 has managed to guess the number of CPUs in our computer, in my case, this is an iMac with four cores, as shown in the following screenshot:

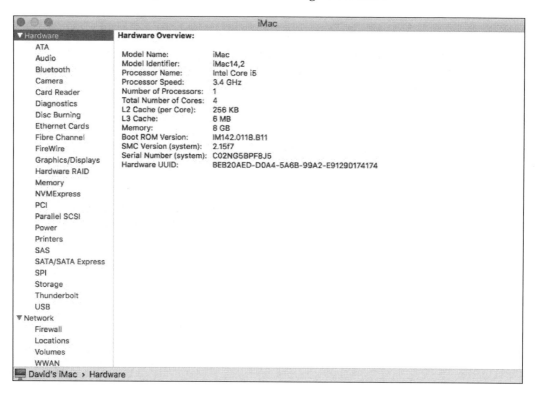

As you can see in `pstree`, PM2 started four threads at the OS level, as shown in the following image:

When clustering an application, there is an unwritten rule about the number of cores that an application should be using and this number is the number of cores minus one.

The reason behind this number is the fact that the OS needs some CPU power so that if we use all the CPUs in our application, once the OS starts carrying on with some other tasks, it will force context switching as all the cores will be busy and this will slow down the application.

Load balancing our application

Sometimes, clustering our app is not enough and we need to scale our application horizontally.

There are a number of ways to horizontally scale an app. Nowadays, with cloud providers such as Amazon, every single provider has implemented their own solution with a number of features.

One of my preferred ways of implementing the load balancing is using **NGINX**.

NGINX is a web server with a strong focus on the concurrency and low memory usage. It is also the perfect fit for Node.js applications as it is highly discouraged to serve static resources from within a Node.js application. The main reason is to avoid the application from being under stress due to a task that could be done better with another software, such as NGINX (which is another example of specialization).

However, let's focus on load balancing. The following figure shows how NGINX works as a load balancer:

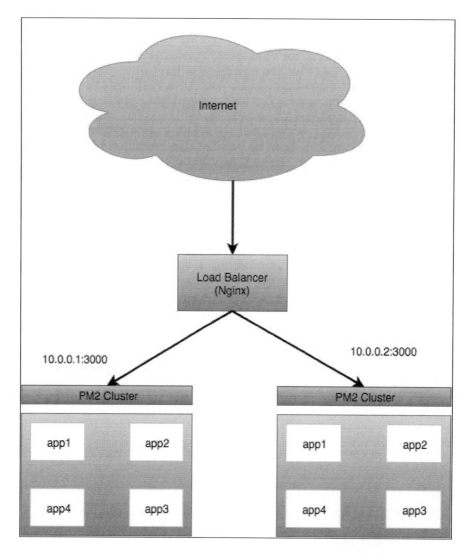

As you can see in the preceding diagram, we have two PM2 clusters load balanced by an instance of NGINX.

The first thing we need to do is know how NGINX manages the configuration.

On Linux, NGINX can be installed via yum, apt-get, or any other package manager. It can also be built from the source, but the recommended method, unless you have very specific requirements, is to use a package manager.

By default, the main configuration file is `/etc/nginx/nginx.conf`, as follows:

```
user    nginx;
worker_processes    1;

error_log  /var/log/nginx/error.log warn;
pid         /var/run/nginx.pid;

events {
  worker_connections  1024;
}

http {
  include                   /etc/nginx/mime.types;
  default_type              application/octet-stream;

  log_format          main '$remote_addr - $remote_user [$time_local]
      "$request" '
      '$status $body_bytes_sent "$http_referer" '
      '"$http_user_agent" "$http_x_forwarded_for" '
      '$request_time';

  access_log                /var/log/nginx/access.log   main;
  server_tokens             off;
  sendfile                  on;
  #tcp_nopush               on;
  keepalive_timeout         65s;
  send_timeout              15s;
  client_header_timeout     15s;
  client_body_timeout       15s;
  client_max_body_size      5m;
  ignore_invalid_headers    on;
  fastcgi_buffers           16 4k;
  #gzip                     on;
  include                   /etc/nginx/sites-enabled/*.conf;
}
```

This file is pretty straightforward, it specifies the number of workers (remember, processes to serve requests), the location of error logs, number connections that a worker can have active at the time, and finally, the HTTP configuration.

The last line is the most interesting one: we are informing NGINX to use `/etc/nginx/sites-enabled/*.conf` as potential configuration files.

With this configuration, every file ending in `.conf` under the specified folder is going to be part of the NGINX configuration.

As you can see, there is a default file already existing there. Modify it to look as follows:

```
http {
  upstream app {
    server 10.0.0.1:3000;
    server 10.0.0.2:3000;
  }
  server {
    listen 80;
    location / {
      proxy_pass http://app;
    }
  }
}
```

This is all the configuration we need to build a load balancer. Let's explain it in the following:

- The `upstream app` directive is creating a group of services called `app`. Inside this directive, we specify two servers as we've seen in the previous image.
- The `server` directive specifies to NGINX that it should be listening to all the requests from port `80` and passing them to the group of upstream called `app`.

Now, how does NGINX decide to send the request to which computer?

In this case, we could specify the strategy used to spread the load.

By default, NGINX, when there is not a balancing method specifically configured, uses **Round Robin**.

One thing to bear in mind is that if we use round robin, our application should be stateless as we won't be always hitting the same machine, so if we save the status in the server, it might not be there in the following call.

Round Robin is the most elementary way of distributing load from a queue of work into a number of workers; it rotates them so that every node gets the *same amount of requests*.

There are other mechanisms to spread the load, as follows:

```
upstream app {
  least_conn;
  server 10.0.0.1:3000;
  server 10.0.0.2:3000;
}
```

Least connected, as its name indicates, sends the request to the least connected node, equally distributing the load between all the nodes:

```
upstream app {
  ip_hash;
  server 10.0.0.1:3000;
  server 10.0.0.2:3000;
}
```

IP hashing is an interesting way of distributing the load. If you have ever worked with any web application, the concept of sessions is something present in almost any application. In order to remember who the user is, the browser sends a cookie to the server, which has stored who the user is in memory and what data he/she needs/can be accessed by that given user. The problem with the other type of load balancing is that we are not guaranteed to always hit the same server.

For example, if we are using Least connected as a policy for balancing, we could hit the server one in the first load, but then hit a different server on subsequent redirections that will result in the user not being displayed with the right information as the second server won't know who the user is.

With IP hashing, the load balancer will calculate a hash for a given IP. This hash will somehow result in a number from 1 to N, where N is the number of servers, and then, the user will always be redirected to the same machine as long as they keep the same IP.

We can also apply a weight to the load balancing, as follows:

```
upstream app {
  server 10.0.0.1:3000 weight=5;
  server 10.0.0.2:3000;
}
```

This will distribute the load in such way that, for every six requests, five will be directed to the first machine and one will be directed to the second machine.

Once we have chosen our preferred load balancing method, we can restart NGINX for the changes to take effect, but first, we want to validate them as shown in the following image:

```
vagrant@dgonzalez-vagrant ~ $ sudo /etc/init.d/nginx configtest
nginx: the configuration file /etc/nginx/nginx.conf syntax is ok
nginx: configuration file /etc/nginx/nginx.conf test is successful
vagrant@dgonzalez-vagrant ~ $
```

As you can see, the configuration test can be really helpful in order to avoid configuration disasters.

Once NGINX has passed `configtest`, it is guaranteed that NGINX will be able to `restart/start/reload` without any syntax problem, as follows:

```
sudo /etc/init.d/nginx reload
```

Reload will gracefully wait until the old threads are done, and then, reload the configuration and route the new requests with the new configuration.

If you are interested in learning about NGINX, I found the following official documentation of NGINX quite helpful:

```
http://nginx.org/en/docs/
```

Health check on NGINX

Health checking is one of the important activities on a load balancer. What happens if one of the nodes suffers a critical hardware failure and is unable to serve more requests?

In this case, NGINX comes with two types of health checks: **passive** and **active**.

Passive health check

Here, NGINX is configured as a reverse proxy (as we did in the preceding section). It reacts to a certain type of response from the upstream servers.

If there is an error coming back, NGINX will mark the node as faulty, removing it from the load balancing for a certain period of time before reintroducing it. With this strategy, the number of failures will be drastically reduced as NGINX will be constantly removing the node from the load balancer.

There are a few configurable parameters, such as `max_fails` or `fail_timeout`, where we can configure the amount of failures required to mark a node as invalid or the time out for requests.

Active health check

Active health checks, unlike passive health checks, actively issue connections to the upstream servers to check whether they are responding correctly to the experiencing problems.

The most simplistic configuration for active health checks in NGINX is the following one:

```
http {
  upstream app {
    zone app test;
    server 10.0.0.1:3000;
    server 10.0.0.2:3000;
  }
  server {
    listen 80;
    location / {
      proxy_pass http://app;
      health_check;
    }
  }
}
```

There are two new lines in this config file, as follows:

- `health_check`: This enables the active health check. The default configuration is to issue a connection every five seconds to the host and port specified in the `upstream` section.

- `zone app test`: This is required by the NGINX configuration when enabling the health check.

There is a wide range of options to configure more specific health checks, and all of them are available in NGINX configuration that can be combined to satisfy the needs of different users.

Summary

In this chapter, you learned a wide range of technologies that we can use to deploy microservices. By now you know how to build, deploy, and configure software components in such a way that we are able to homogenize a very diverse range of technologies. The objective of this book is to provide you the concepts required to start working with microservices and enable the reader to know how to look for the needed information.

Personally, I have struggled to find a book that provides a summary of all the aspects of the life cycle of microservices and I really hope that this book covers this empty space.

Index

I

independence 18
infrastructure logical security 131, 132
injection
  about 136-138
  input validation 138
input validation 138, 139
integration tests 156
IP hashing 257

J

Java Remote Method Invocation (RMI) 12
JavaScript 32, 33
JavaScript Object Notation (JSON) 80
JSON 192

K

key benefits
  easy to deploy 18
  independence 18
  replaceability 17
  resilience 13
  scalability 14, 15
  technology heterogeneity 15, 16
key design principles
  about 4
  business units 5-7
  decentralization 9-11
  small size 12
  smart services 8, 9
  technology alignment 12
Keymetrics
  about 202
  custom metrics 214
  URL 202, 206
  used, for diagnosing problems 207-212
  used, for monitoring application
     exceptions 212-214
  used, for monitoring services 202-206

L

latency 221
Latency Monkey 220
least connected node 257

libuv library 244

load balancing
  of Node.js applications 253-258
logging 145-147
logging, levels
  DEBUG 149
  ERROR 149
  FATAL 149
  INFO 149
  WAR 149
loosely coupled business unit 6

M

Mandrill
  integrating, in microservice 94-97
  setting up 92-94
  URL 92-96
manual testing
  about 184
  Postman 185-189
  proxy, building to debug microservices 184
memory leak 207
micromerce
  about 77
  deploying, PM2 used 229
microservices
  APIs, documenting with Swagger 189-197
  disadvantages 71
  documenting 189
  evolution 64-70
  in real world 2, 3
  monolith, splitting 71, 72
  need for 1
  project, generating from Swagger
     definition 197-199
  small size microservices 12
  testing 173, 174
  testing, in Node.js 160
  versus Service-Oriented Architectures
     (SOA) 19, 20
microservices-oriented architectures
  about 3
  benefits 3
  shortcomings 3, 4
Mocha 160, 165

Printed in Great Britain
by Amazon